Two Antiquaries

Two Antiquaries

A Selection from the Correspondence of John Aubrey and Anthony Wood

Maurice Balme

Durham Academic Press
Edinburgh – Cambridge – Durham – USA

First published in 2001 by
Durham Academic Press
1 Hutton Close
South Church
Bishop Auckland
Durham

Email: manuscripts@pentlandpress.co.uk
Web: pentlandpress.co.uk

ISBN 1-900838-11-7

Typeset in Bell 11 on 13
by Carnegie Publishing,
Carnegie House,
Chatsworth Road,
Lancaster

www.carnegiepub.co.uk

Printed and bound by
Antony Rowe Ltd,
Chippenham

The author gratefully acknowledges and gives thanks to the Oxford Historical Society for their kind permission to reproduce extracts from A. Clark's *The Life and Times of Anthony Wood.*

Contents

Illustrations

Foreword

EVERYONE IS ASTONISHED by the apparent incompatibilities of love. 'What *can* he see in her?' But friendship, as this fascinating correspondence demonstrates is no less perplexing. Any two natures, at first sight more disparate than the genial, tolerant, amusing Aubrey and the crabbed, prickly, censorious Wood would be hard to find. Yet, as Maurice Balme in a subtle exploration of their characters suggests, they were not so far apart as the generally received view has taken them to be. Wood, closely examined, proves to be a jollier, more convivial figure than appears from the often-quoted nagging and complaining of his journals. And when Aubrey, a much richer man, has squandered and muddled away his inheritance Wood occasionally accompanies his gritty, persistent letters with a useful remittance. Aubrey, on the other hand, for all his heart-warming generosity to fellow-scholars who plundered and plagiarised his work, is here shown to have treated his own brother with meanness and dishonesty.

More powerful than any personal attraction was their common passion for rescuing the evidences of the past from what Aubrey called 'the teeth of time'. Wood's myopic single-mindness, sticking through thick and thin to his history of Oxford University and its alumni, counterpointed Aubrey's exuberant, wide-ranging curiosity about everything and everybody. Without Wood's relentless questioning we would not have Aubrey's glittering answers. There is no comparison between the originality, breadth and vivacity of his mind, the champagne of his language, and the flat obviousness of his correspondent. But they perform a double act in the same literary class as Holmes and Watson or Jeeves and Bertie Wooster.

Inevitably Aubrey captivates the reader. Every turn of his mind, every inflection of his prose, seizes our attention. He is so intensely a man of his age, the personification of the Royal Society, the friend of Hooke and Sir Christopher Wren, of writers as different as Dryden and Sir Thomas Browne, and yet, of all seventeenth-century figures, he seems, as Anthony Powell pointed out in *John Aubrey and his Friends*, the closest to modern sensibilities. Considering the various options of restoring his fallen fortunes he rejects the Church, in which he would easily have obtained preferment, on the grounds that he would look, and feel, absurd in a cassock. Even more out of tune with his times and in tune with ours is his sudden use of Wood's Christian name: 'In the interim I rest in Hast, deare Anthony, your most affectionate and obliged friend and servant.' He does not often use this form. Usually it is 'Deare Friend' or 'Mr Woodes', the cavalier spelling of proper names so characteristic of the century. But to use it at all is surprising when even the most intimate letters prefer endearment: 'Sweetheart', 'my deare love', 'little rogue' to the Christian name.

Aubrey's interest and proficiency in fields of learning unknown to Wood has been comprehensively demonstrated in Michael Hunter's *John Aubrey and the Realm of Learning*. He was, and knew himself to be, the founder of the modern scientific study of archaeology. But, as these letters show, contemporary life supplies material to the wit that, in his own words, was 'alwaies working'. How many of his friends observed, as he did, the importance of coffee-houses as social and intellectual catalysts, the equivalent in their day of railways in Victorian Britain and of the Internet in ours? In a letter of 15 June 1680 he remarks on 'the modern advantage of coffee-houses in this great citie, before which men knew not how to be acquainted, but with their own relations or societies'.

This civilised, detached, sceptical curiosity had to accommodate itself to a society in which these qualities carried their own dangers. Pepys kept his diary in shorthand that not everyone could read and secreted it under lock and key. The freedom of its expression could have cost its writer dear. Aubrey, much less astute than his fellow-member of the Royal Society, was yet well aware that much of the information that he communicated to Wood could land him in serious trouble.

He was also alive to the possibilities, even, as it seemed to him, the probabilities of violent political change. What that meant for the preservation of irreplaceable documents he had known from his childhood when philistine parsons were still using manuscripts pillaged from monastic libraries at the Dissolution to line pie-dishes or stop up the bungs of cider barrels. As a young man he had seen the wanton destruction of great collections in the Civil War. These were lessons he never forgot. Incompetent as he was at managing his everyday affairs, the care and forethought he showed in far greater measure than Wood have yielded us treasures of which the present volume offers an irresistible selection.

Richard Ollard

Introduction

THE CORRESPONDENCE OF JOHN AUBREY AND ANTHONY WOOD lasted, with a few hiatuses, from 1668, the year after they first met, until Wood's death in 1695. Over 180 letters from Aubrey to Wood survive and about twenty from Wood to Aubrey. Throughout this time Wood was engaged in writing first the History of Oxford University, which included brief notices of distinguished Oxford alumni (published 1674), and then *Athenae Oxonienses*, over 2,000 lives of Oxford men (published 1693–4). Wood bombarded Aubrey with queries about the men on whom he was writing and Aubrey replied with long rambling letters in which he not only answered Wood's queries but poured forth his innermost thoughts. We not only learn of his activities and feelings month by month and year by year but also acquire an insight into his complex character and his extraordinary resilience in the face of adversity. The letters throw a fascinating light on the life and character of both Aubrey and Wood, especially the former, who was known to the world almost entirely through his *Brief Lives* until the publication of Anthony Powell's *John Aubrey and his Friends* (1963) and Michael Hunter's *John Aubrey and the Realm of Learning* (1975), which places him in his intellectual context and shows the important contributions he made to learning, especially in archaeology. Much is omitted, above all the part he played in the early years of the Royal Society through his close friendship with Robert Hooke and other leading members, but from these letters we come to know Aubrey better then any man of the seventeenth century except Pepys.

The letters are preserved in the Bodleian Library. Aubrey entrusted all his manuscripts and papers to Edward Llwyd, keeper of the Ashmolean Museum, in 1693. Amongst these were two folio volumes of letters to Aubrey (A12,13), including a number from Wood. All Wood's multifarious papers and letters were consigned to the Ashmolean on his death. Both collections were later acquired by the Bodleian. In 1693, when Wood was in trouble for libelling the Earl of Clarendon in his *Athenae Oxonienses*, he asked Aubrey to return all his letters in case they contained incriminating material. Aubrey sent him all but a few, which he could not find. These are retained in Aubrey's collection of letters but the remainder are lost, presumably destroyed by Wood. Wood, on the other hand, although Aubrey asked for the return of his letters, kept them all. Consequently the correspondence is one-sided; we have all (?) Aubrey's letters to Wood, but only a few from Wood to Aubrey. A fair number of Aubrey's letters are found in other collections in the Bodleian, those of Ashmole, Ballard and Tanner, who were all voluminous collectors.

In our commentary we often quote from Aubrey's autobiographical notes (A7, folios 3–5), which he included in the manuscript of *Brief Lives*, and from his Accidents (a list of significant events in his life) (Ballard 14, 158–9). We make frequent use of Wood's Autobiography and Journal, which are published in full in A. Clark's *Wood's Life and Times*. Appendix I contains a list of Aubrey's works which are referred to from time to time and of Wood's works.

The first two chapters are introductory, giving a brief outline of the lives of the protagonists until the year they met. Thereafter the letters are quoted in chronological order with a running commentary. Aubrey uses old-style year datings, that is to say his new year begins on 25 March; to avoid confusion we have always given new-style datings.

Most of these letters are quoted in whole or in part by Anthony Powell and Michael Hunter in the works referred to above, and also by David Tylden-Wright in *John Aubrey, A Life* (HarperCollins 1991), but some have never been published before; and here it is right that I should acknowledge my debt to Dr James Williams, who made an annotated transcript of all Aubrey's correspondence with Wood and Llwyd, a massive work of scholarship, unfortunately never published; access to this typescript (a D.Phil thesis for London University) has saved me many hours of searching and transcribing in the Bodleian Library. I must also express my gratitude to the Keeper of Western Manuscripts and the staff of the Bodleian for the courtesy and efficiency with which they have invariably produced these priceless manuscripts for me to read and transcribe.

Abbreviations used in references:

B.L. = *Brief Lives*, A. Clark's edition in two volumes (Oxford, 1898); references are either to the life, e.g. B.L. Hooke, or by volume and page.

L & T = A. Clark, *Wood's Life and Times*, in four volumes (Oxford Historical Society 1884–95).

Auto = Aubrey's autobiographical note as in Clark B.L. i, pages 24–45.

T.P.W. = *Three Prose Works*, J. Buchanan-Brown, Centaur Press, 1972.

This includes *The Miscellanies, The Remaines of Gentilisme and Judaism, and Observations* (notes by Aubrey preserved in the Classified Papers and Letter Books of the Royal Society).

Hunter = Michael Hunter, *John Aubrey and the Realm of Learning*, Duckworth, 1975.

Chapter 1

John Aubrey 1626–1667

JOHN AUBREY FIRST MET ANTHONY WOOD on 31 August 1667, when he was aged forty-one and already well advanced on the slippery slope which was to lead to destitution. He was born on 12 March 1626 at Easton Piers in Wiltshire at the house of his grandfather, Isaac Lyte, where he lived for the first ten years of his life. At birth he was 'very weak and like to die, that I was christned before morning prayer'. (Auto) He had a lonely childhood: 'when a boy, bred at Easton, an eremiticall solitude' (Auto); his younger brothers, William and Tom, were not born until he was already at Oxford. 'I was,' he says, 'inclin'd by my Genius, from my Childhood to the love of Antiquities.' He loved to listen to the stories of his grandfather about times of old, and at an early age was saddened by the wanton destruction of antiquities: 'I remember the Rector here (at Yatton Kenyell), Mr Wiliam Stump, had severall manuscripts of the Abbey (sc. Malmesbury Abbey). He was a proper Man and a good Fellow, and when he brewed a barrell of Speciall Ale, his use was to stop the bung-hole (under the clay) with a sheet of Manuscript; he sayd nothing did it so well; which methought did grieve me to see.'

His health did not improve until at the age of twelve he was sent to Blandford School in Dorset, where he spent four unhappy years but became the best scholar there. When he was sixteen, he went up to Trinity College, Oxford, where he at last found happiness. In his autobiographical notes he gives a sketch of his character at this time:

> I did not very much care for Grammar. I had apprehension enough, but Memorie not tenacious. So that was then a promising morne enough of an inventive and philosophicall head. I had a musicall head, inventive, wrote blank verse, had a strong and early impulse to antiquitie. My wit was alwaies working, but not adroit for verse. I was exceedingly mild of spirit; mightily susceptible of fascination. My idea very clear; phansie like a mirrour, pure chrystal water, which the least wind does disorder and unsmooth.

The Oxford which he joined was undergoing a revolution. The old certainties were failing in every sphere: 'The new Philosophie calls all in doubt,' Donne had written forty years earlier and now the pace of intellectual change had quickened. The traditional syllabus of Rhetoric, Logic and Ethics was still the norm, but a new wind was blowing from outside the university: Bacon's *Novum Organum*, advocating the study of things rather than words, had been published in 1620; William Harvey's book on the circulation of the blood had come out in 1628, Galileo's *Dialogo*, in which he argues for the Copernican system, in 1630. Many of the Fellows were already eager followers of the new philosophy, including several at Trinity. Before long a brilliant group, which included Ralph Bathurst (later one of the most distinguished presidents of Trinity), Robert Boyle (the father of modern chemistry),

Portrait of John Aubrey aged 40 by William Fairthorne, by kind permission of the Curator, Ashmolean Museum, Oxford

Robert Hooke (see page 11), William Petty (Professor of Anatomy at Oxford and the first political economist), Seth Ward (Savilian Professor of Geometry at Oxford and later Bishop of Salisbury), John Wilkins (Warden of Wadham and first Secretary of the Royal Society; later Bishop of Chester), and Christopher Wren, were to take the lead with the foundation of the Oxford Experimental Philosophical Club, from which the Royal Society later developed.

Aubrey was quickly drawn towards the new philosophy, dismissing the traditional syllabus summarily ('Looked through Logique and some Ethiques'). He became convinced that 'Arithmetic and Geometrie are the keys which open unto us all mathematicall and philosphicall knowledge,' (A10, 8), but he never excelled in this sphere and he eventually gave up the scientific experiments which he started making at Oxford and continued after he had gone down. He read widely, including books on mathematics and astronomy, and made friends amongst men who were to be prominent in the new learning, above all, John Hoskyns, who remained devoted to him throughout his life; he shared Aubrey's interests and was later President of the Royal Society. A number of his letters to Aubrey survive, which give a vivid picture of their social life in the 1660s and show a deep concern for Aubrey when he became destitute, ever ready with help and advice.

Other Trinity men with whom he formed lifelong friendships and from whom letters survive were Anthony Etterick (1622–1703), who followed him to the Middle Temple and was later Recorder of Poole and MP for Christchurch; and Thomas Mariet, with whom Aubrey shared rooms at the time of the Restoration when Mariet was secretly negotiating for the King's return; he was High Sheriff of Warwickshire at the time of the Popish plot and arrested Ralph Sheldon with whom Wood was staying (see p. 76). Nor should Ralph Kettell be omitted, the formidable President of Trinity who had held this office for nearly fifty years when Aubrey first went up: 'His gowne and surplice and hood being on, he had a terrible gigantique aspect, with his sharp gray eyes' (B.L. Kettell). He made a deep impression on Aubrey who devoted one of the longest *Lives* to him and several times refers to him in his letters. 'He was an excellent governour …when he scolded at the idle boies of his college, he used these names, viz. Turds, Tarrarags (these were the worst sort, rude rakells), Rascal-Jacks, Blindcinques, Scobberlotches (these did no hurt, were sober, but went idleing about the grove with their hands in their pockets, and telling the number of the trees there, or so).' Aubrey refers to himself as a 'scobberlotcher' in a letter to Wood many years later (see page?). Lastly, he was a friend of Anthony Wood's elder brother Edward, who had a room above the gate of Trinity, a 'cockleloft', to which Anthony went every day for tuition; so the paths of Aubrey and Wood may have crossed twenty years before they became acquainted.

When the Civil War began (August 1642), 'my father sent for me home for feare'. The following February 'with much adoe I gott my father to lett me to beloved Oxon againe, then a garrison pro rege' (Auto). But in June he was unlucky enough to contract smallpox and when he recovered, returned home once more, now Broad Chalke Manor Farm near Salisbury, where he spent a miserable time for the next three years: 'Twas a most sad life for me, in the prime of my life not to have the benefitt of an ingeniose conversation and scarce any good bookes – almost a consumption ...This sad life I did lead in the country till 1646, at which time I gott (with much adoe) leave of my father to lett me goe to the Middle Temple; April 6th, 1646 admitted.' 'Then, November 1646, I returned to Trinity College in Oxon again to my great joy; was made much of by the Fellowes; had their learned conversation. lookt on bookes, musique. Here, and at the Middle Temple (off and on) I (for the most part) enjoyed the greatest felicity of my life (ingeniose youths, as rosebudds, imbibe the morning dew)' (Auto).

But this happiness was not to last. 'December 1648 (Christmas Eve's eve) I was sent from Oxon home again to my sick father, who never recovered; where I was engaged to looke after his country business and solicite a law-suit.'

Richard Aubrey had inherited two estates in Herefordshire and the estate at Broad Chalke, which had been held by his family on lease from the Earls of Pembroke since 1601. But his health was weak and he seems to have been incompetent; when he died in 1652, he bequeathed to his son little but debts which the latter was never able to pay off. The country business Aubrey had to look after would have been not only the farm at Broad Chalke but also the management of the estates in Herefordshire; he was singularly incompetent in this sphere and wrote many years later that he was predestinated to be 'cousened and cheated'. The lawsuit which Aubrey had to undertake was interminable; it was an attempt to claim some lands in Wales which had belonged to his great-great-grandfather, William Aubrey, a distinguished minister of Queen Elizabeth. Aubrey persevered in this suit for many years (he was still engaged in it when he met Wood in 1667) and lost a fortune in its pursuit.

But at Christmas 1648 he was not unduly concerned with these irksome duties. No sooner had he returned home, than he was off to Marlborough to stay with Charles Seymour, where his visit resulted in a momentous discovery which was to influence the remainder of his life.

The morrow after twelf day Mr Charles Seymour and Sir William

> Tokenham, baronet, met with their pack of hounds at the Grey Wethers ...'Twas here that our game began and the chase led us at length thorough the village of Aubury (= Avebury) into the closes there: where I was wonderfully surprised at the sight of those vast stones ...I left the company awhile, entertaining myself with a more delighfull indagation: and then steered by the cry of the hounds I overtook the company and went with them to Kynnet, where a good hunting dinner was provided. (*Templa Druidum*, Preface)

Aubrey had been fascinated by antiquities of every kind ever since he was a child but his visit to Avebury, which was at this time virtually unknown, roused his interest to a higher pitch and led eventually to his most important work, *Monumenta Britannica*.

While he vegetated at Broad Chalke, he maintained contact with Oxford by correspondence, especially with John Lydall, a young fellow of Trinity who was a keen follower of the new philosophy and a member of the Oxford Experimental Philosophical Club. Several of his letters to Aubrey survive which show how highly he was valued at Oxford; in one, written on 20 February 1649, he says: 'Mr Aubrey, it is our unhappiness as well as yours that you are deprived of the comfort of your studys and of your friends here, who must ever be engaged for this your remembrance and esteeme of them, and must ever account you as one borne for the honour and preservation of learning' (A12, 298). In September Lydall wrote promising to keep him in touch with any discoveries made by the Club.

The next year he formed a new friendship with another Trinity man, Francis Potter, younger brother of the President of the college, a brilliant mechanic, interested in such questions as astronomy, flying machines and submarines, and the first to attempt experiments in blood transfusion, which were later taken up by the Royal Society. He and Aubrey often stayed with each other and they conducted a massive correspondence ('I have all his letters by me, and I beleeve neer 200, and most of them philosophicall'); many of these survive in Aubrey's collection of philosophical letters.

Following his father's death, Aubrey had greater freedom; he was, to all appearances, a wealthy landowner and for some years he lived like one. He planned to travel to Italy to see the antiquities but these plans fell through when none of his friends could join him and his mother 'to my inexpressible griefe and ruine, hindred this designe' (Auto). His home was now Broad Chalke, the lease of which he had taken on when his father died, but he kept the law terms in London where he had lodgings in Fleet Street. He made little progress in the law but letters from friends such as Sir John Hoskyns show him enjoying a busy social and intellectual life. By now most members of the Oxford Philosophical Club had moved to London and he numbered amongst his friends Hooke, Petty, Wren and Boyle; it was also at this time that he got to know the philosopher Thomas Hobbes, who became a close friend.

Out of term his life was consumed by continual and ineffectual activity: 'Then (i.e. after the failure of his plan to travel to Italy) debts and lawe-suits, borrowing of money, and perpetual riding'. His 'perpetual riding' was from Broad Chalke to Easton Piers, to Brecon and Monmouthshire in pursuit of his claim to lands there, to Herefordshire to see to his estates. It was on these interminable journeys ('never off horseback') that he began to make notes on antiquities and natural history: 'He began to enter into pocket memorandum bookes philosophicall and antiquarian remarques Anno Domini 1654' (Auto); 'My head was alwaies working; never idle; and even travelling did gleane some observations, of which I have a collection in folio of 2 quiers of paper + a dust basket' (Auto). In 1656 he began to arrange and expand some of these into what was to become his *Natural History of Wiltshire*. Four years later he embarked on his first antiquarian project, the 'Wiltshire Antiquities', which eventually filled two massive books but remained unfinished.

All this time his debts were mounting and he was continually borrowing: 'To my prayse, I had wonderfull credit in the countrey for money', but he was shortly reduced to selling his Stretford estate in Herefordshire; he made a bad bargain and any financial relief was temporary. In 1661, at the age of 35, taking stock of his life, he was singularly dissatisfied: 'What have I done worthwhile at this stage of my life? Truly nothing; only umbrages …' (Auto).

But the foundation of the Royal Society in 1662 was to give him a new lease of life. He was elected an original Fellow in January 1663; from the time of his election it became the centre of his life and he never missed a meeting if he could help it. He was soon on good terms with many of the Fellows; it would be no exaggeration to say that through his constant attendance at the Society's meetings he became acquainted with all the leading intellectuals of the day. For Aubrey the Society was 'our club', and after the weekly meetings, he usually adjourned with a group of friends to a coffee house, where discussion continued, often till late at night. 'It haz been a Ferment to the inventive heads of the World. By this way Knowledge will make a greater shoote in 10 yeares then it did before in a hundred' (A3 18v). Among the closest friends he made amongst the Fellows was Robert Hooke; he had been Boyle's assistant at Oxford but when the Royal Society was formed, he was made Curator of Experiments with rooms in Gresham

College, where the Society met regularly on Wednesday afternoons. He had to 'furnish the Society every daye they meete with three or four considerable experiments'; this he did for many years, covering an astonishingly wide field of scientific inquiry – light, combustion, the microscope, astronomy. Aubrey had unstinted admiration for him: 'As he is of a prodigious inventive head, so he is a person of great vertue and goodness ...He is certainly the greatest mechanick this day in the world' (B.L. Hooke). In 1674 Aubrey moved into rooms within a stone's throw of Gresham College and often helped Hooke in the preparation of his experiments, spending whole days together with him and perhaps at one time even sharing his rooms.

At a meeting on 8 July 1663 the Avebury monuments were discussed and Aubrey was asked to investigate them further. The President, Lord Brouncker, mentioned Avebury to the King, reporting that Aubrey had said that Avebury 'did as much excell Stoneheng as a cathedral doth a Parish church'. The King wanted to hear more and sent for Aubrey, who brought him a sketch of Avebury.

> His Majestie was pleased, gave me his hand to kiss, and commanded me to waite on him at Marleborough, when he went to Bath with the Queen (which was about a fortnight after), which I did: and the next day, when the Court were on their journey, his Majestie left the Queen and diverted to Aubury (29 August), where I shewed him that stupendious Antiquity, with a view wherof he and his Royal Highness the Duke of York were very well pleased. His Majestie then commanded me to write a Description of it and present it to him: and the Duke of Yorke commanded me to give an account of the Old Camps and Barrows on the Plaines ... In September following I surveyed the old Monument of Aubury with a plaine table, and afterwards tooke a Review of Stoneheng, and then I composed this following discourse in obedience to his Majestie's command: and presented it to him: which he commanded me to print. (*Templa Druidum*, Preface)

This must have been a happy and productive time for Aubrey, but debts continued to mount and later that year he was forced to sell his other Herefordshire estate to Thomas Willis, an old Oxford friend and a distinguished doctor and chemist. In the summer of 1664 Aubrey at last achieved his ambition of travelling on the continent, but the trip proved something of a fiasco: 'June 11, landed at Calais. In August following, had a terrible fit of the spleen, and piles, at Orleans. I returned in October' (Accidents). He travelled with George Ent, whom he refers to in a letter to Wood as my 'old acquaintance and fellow traveller' (August 1674, Ballard 14, 107). Ent was the elder son of Sir George Ent F.R.S., a distinguished physician. He was an uncouth character, often drunk and much given to 'rhodomontades', but despite his faults Aubrey remained unfailingly loyal to him.

The years following his trip to France were disastrous for Aubrey. Of 1666 he says: 'this yeare all my businesses and affairs ran kim kam. Nothing tooke effect, as if I had been under an ill tongue. Treacheries and enmities in abundance against me' (Accidents). Now aged forty, he had only once been deeply in love: '1651: about the 16 or 18 of April, I sawe that incomparable good conditioned gentlewoman, Mrs M. Wiseman, with whom at first sight I was in love.' He remained faithful to her for five years but she married another. He then became engaged to a wealthy girl, Katherine Ryves, who died shortly before they were to be married (1657). Now the only way he could see out of his financial straits was to marry a rich girl: '1665 November 1: I made my first addresse (in an ill houre) to Joan Sumner' (Accidents). The Sumners were wealthy clothiers. There was no question of this being a love match: Aubrey would win by it financial security, Joan social promotion. But the affair went disastrously wrong; Joan broke off the engagement and Aubrey brought an action against her for breach of promise. He eventually won this action and received £300 damages but the dispute lingered on as Joan claimed the repayment of some bonds and the case was not finally settled until April 1670.

It was while the Joan Sumner affair was at its height that Aubrey first met Anthony Wood on 31 August 1667.

Chapter II

Anthony Wood 1632–1667

ANTHONY WOOD WAS BORN IN 1632 in Postmasters Hall, Merton Street, Oxford and died there in 1695. His father, Thomas Wood, was a prosperous man, who owned, besides the lease of Postmasters Hall, an inn in Oxford called the Fleur de Luce, and land in Tetsworth and elsewhere. By his second wife Mary Petty he had six sons, of whom Anthony was the fourth. His early years were uneventful. When he was nine he was sent to New College school. The next year saw the beginning of the Civil War. Soon Oxford became the Royalist head-quarters and was packed to bursting with the court and regiments continually coming and going. In November (1642), Postmasters Hall was commandeered by the Master of the Rolls and Wood's family moved out into a smaller house. At the same time the buildings occupied by New College school became a magazine and the school was moved into 'a dark nasty room, very unfit for such a purpose'. Wood's autobiography gives a vivid picture of these chaotic and dangerous days.

In January 1643 his father died. The following year, when there was plague in Oxford and danger that the city might be besieged, Wood's mother decided to send him and his younger brother Christopher out of the city to Thame; there they stayed with the vicar Thomas Henant, whose wife was a distant relative, and went to Lord William's Free School. The boys were 'very lovingly received' by the vicar and his wife, though Anthony cannot have been an easy charge.

> He was very sedulous, was alwaies up and readie first in the house, and alwaies ambitious of being first in the school in the morning; and if in any way hindred, he would be apt to cry and make a noise to the disturbance of the house ... A. Wood did partly remember that he was much retired, walked mostly alone, was given much to thinking and to melancholy; which sometimes made his night's rest so much disturbed, that he would walk in his sleep and disturb and fright people of the house. (L & T i, 108–9)

In September 1646 his mother, who had suffered considerable financial loss in a great fire in Oxford, decided she could no longer afford to keep Anthony and Christopher at Thame and sent their brother Edward to say that they were to return to Oxford: 'A.W. seemed very sorry at this news, because he was well and warm where he was, had

Portrait of Anthony Wood aged 48 by Poole, by kind permission of the Bodleian Library, University of Oxford

good companie, and seemed to have a fixed love for the place …But there was no remedy, for go he must and go he did with his brother after Michaelmas following' (L & T i, 129).

On his return 'he found Oxford empty as to scholars, but pretty well replenished with parliamentarian soldiers … but as for the young men of the city and university he found many of them to have been debauch'd by bearing armes and doing the duties belonging to soldiers, as watching, warding, and sitting in tippling houses for whole nights together' (ibid).

Back in Oxford he was tutored by Edward, a scholar of Trinity College, 'to whom he went once or twice a day to receive instruction, and alwaies spent every afternoon in his chamber, which was a cockleloft over the common gate of that college'. The following year he was matriculated and became a gentleman commoner of Merton College. He spent five undistinguished years as an undergraduate. In April 1648, called before the Parliamentary visitors nominated for 'the better regulating and Reformation of the University of Oxford', he was nearly expelled for refusing to submit to the authority of Parliament: 'Called in he was ask'd this question by one of the Visitors: "Will you submit to the authority of Parliament in this visitation?" To which he gave this answer, and wrot it down on a paper lying on the table: "I do not understand this business, and therefore I am not able to give a direct answer."'

Afterwards his mother and brother Edward, who advised him to submit in plain terms, were exceedingly angry with him, and told him 'he had ruined himself, and must therefore go a begging' (L & T i, 144). His mother got a friend to intervene and 'he was connived at and kept his place, otherwise he had infallibly gon to the pot'. Throughout his life he was an ardent royalist and had nothing but contempt for Puritans of every colour, whom he called 'sniveling saints'.

His tutor was Edward, now a Fellow of Merton, who found him a backward pupil: 'A. Wood's brother was peevish and would be ever and anon angry if he could not take or understand Logical notions as well as he. He would sometimes be so angry that he would beat him and turn him out of his chamber' (L & T i, 162). He complained to his mother, who arranged for him to have another tutor. He eventually graduated in July 1652 but had no idea what to do next. His mother, anxious for his future, was always 'soliciting him to be an apprentice, which he would never endure to heare of … Nay she was so silly that she would several times propose to him some inferior mechanical trade.'

For a year he led an aimless existence in poor health, but then regained his strength and suddenly found his vocation. In 1653, when he was twenty-one, he was

> entered in the publick library (i.e became a reader in the Bodleian), which

> he took to be the happiness of his life; he was a constant student therein ... Heraldry, musick and painting did so much crowd upon him that he could not avoid them: and could never give a reason why he should delight in those studies more than others, so prevalent was nature, mix'd with a generosity of mind and a hatred to all that was servile, sneaking, or advantagious for lucre sake. (L & T i, 183–4)

Three years later a reading of Dugdale's *Warwickshire* finally confirmed his ambition to become an antiquarian:

> This summer came to Oxon *The Antiquities of Warwickshire etc.* written by William Dugdale ...This being accounted the best book of its kind that hitherto was made extant, my pen cannot enough describe how A. Wood's tender affections and insatiable desire of knowledge were ravish'd and melted downe by the reading of that book. What by musick and rare books that he found in the publick library, his life, at this time and after, was a perfect Elysium. (L & T i, 209)

He immediately started studying the monuments of Oxford and the surrounding countryside, which led in February 1660 to his decision to write a the history of the city and university of Oxford:

> At this time A.W. being resolve'd to set himself to the study of antiquities and do something in them; in the house where he was borne, he set up a chimney in the upper roome looking east; and in the next room joyning he put out a window next to the street, and made it a study, in which he composed for the most part those things which he afterwards published. (L & T i, 304)

He worked in this garret for the rest of his life and died there in 1695; no one was ever admitted to it except Charlett and Tanner on his death bed.

Wood is usually portrayed as a solitary, cross-grained and melancholy man, but the evidence not only of Aubrey's letters but also of Wood's own diary and journal bely this picture. He was certainly not an easy man, always touchy and subject to attacks of spleen, but he was also sociable, spending most evenings of the week with friends in taverns and coffee houses until he was struck with deafness (1670); indeed, Aubrey called the group he met with Wood on his visits to Oxford 'the merry gang'. He was an ardent violinist, who played weekly with a group of the leading musicians of the university: 'All the time that A.W. could spare from his beloved studies of English history, antiquities, heraldry, and genealogies, he spent in the most delightful facultie of musick, either instrumental or vocal: and if he had missed the weekly meeting in the house of William Ellis, he could not well enjoy himself all the week after' (L & T i, 273). He must have been a competent performer, for once, at a music party given by John Wilkins in Wadham College, he found himself playing with the greatest virtuoso of the time, Thomas Baltzar, 'as poor Troilus did against Achilles' (L & T i, 257). Above all, he was happy in the work to which he devoted himself: 'His life, at this time and after, was a perfect Elysium.'

He describes his meeting with Aubrey in a famous passage in his autobiography:

> August 31, Saturday, John Aubrey of Easton Piers in the Parish of Kington S. Michael in Wiltsh. was in Oxon with Edward Forest, a book-seller living against All Souls Coll., to buy books. He then saw lying on the stall *Notitia Acadamiae Oxoniensis*; and asking who the author of that book was, he answer'd the report was that one Mr Anthony Wood of Merton Coll. was the author, but was not (the author was in fact William Fulman). Whereupon Mr Aubrey, a pretender to antiquities, having been contemporary to A. Wood's elder brother in Trin. Coll. and well acquainted with him, he thought that he might be as well acquainted with A.W. himself. Whereupon repairing to his lodgings, and telling him who he was, he got his acquaintance, talk'd to him about his studies, and offer'd what assistance he could make, in order to the completion of the work that he [Wood] was in hand with. Mr Aubrey was then in sparkish garb, came to towne with his man and two horses, spent high, and flung out A.W. at all recknings [i.e. would not let Wood pay his share]. But his estate of 700li per annumn being afterwards sold, and he reserving nothing of it to himself, liv'd afterwards in a very sorry condition, and at length made shift to rub out by hanging on Edmund Wyld esq. living in Blomesbury neare London, on James Bertie earle of Abendon, whose first wife was related to him, and on Sir John Aubrey, his kinsman, living sometimes in Glamorganshire, and sometimes at Borstall neare Brill in Bucks. He was a shiftless person, roving and magotie-headed, and sometimes little better than crased. And being exceedingly credulous, would stuff his many letters sent to A.W. with fooleries, and misinformation, which sometimes would guide him into paths of errour. (L & T ii, 116–17)

Wood must have written this monstrous travesty of their relationship after the great quarrel of 1694, the year before he died, embittered, lonely, sick, and perhaps slightly mad. It is completely misleading on the happy and fruitful cooperation they had enjoyed for over twenty five years. Possibly the only note he made on the meeting at the time was in his diary: 'Aug.31 Thursday, to the barber for cutting my hair, 1s; spent with Mr John Awbrey of Wilts at mother Web's and the Mermaid Tavern, 3s.8d.'; this suggests that they had a convivial evening, and in the course of it Aubrey offered to help Wood in his researches.

Chapter III

'I esteeme myselfe very happy in your acquaintance' 1668–70

SIX WEEKS AFTER THEIR MEETING Wood wrote to Aubrey the first letter in which he asked for information on Oxford worthies whose lives he was including in his history:

Oxon, from my Lodgings against Merton Coll.
Nov.11,1667

Sir,

You may remember when you were at Oxon that you promised upon my inquiries to obtaine some intelligence concerning Dr John Hoskyns some time of New College, of his birth, death and burial, his bookes that he wrote, and what might be worthie memory of him; if you please to informe me as soone as you can, I shall take it for a verie great favoure from your hands. I have some others in mine eye which probably you or some of your acquaintance might satisfie me concerning them; those are Jo. Owen the Epigrammatist and Sr Kenelme Digby; of the first I would only know the time of his death, which is not expressed in his epitaph in the History of Paules (Dugdale); of the other his birth, college or hall in Oxon wherein he was educated, the time of his death, place of sepulcre, and what might be thought fit to be published of soe great a Vertuoso. 'Tis probable you might upon recollection informe me also of others that were Oxford men, the which if you at your leisure can, you would alwaies oblige me to be,

Sr, Yr most humble servant,
Ant.Woode. (A13, 262)

Aubrey was too deeply involved in the Joan Sumner affair to answer at once but he found time to write in January:

Broad Chalke Jan.8th 1668

Sir,

I received yours of Nov.11th at Sarum, just as I was going to London and had these very things with me then that I now make bold to offer to your view, to send you from London. But it is my fate to be plagued with a suite at lawe, that I had not leisure to find this conveyance to you till now.

Concerning the Hoskyns (both the brothers) I shall have exact information the next Terme from the son of the Serjeant at Law ... Concerning Joh. Owen, I can have a full account from his nephew Mr Wil. Clerke of the Check [i.e. the Court of Exchequer], all of which I shall send from London next terme; as also of Sr Kenelme Digby.

I must never forget your kindeness to me at Oxon. I must assure you I esteeme my selfe very happy in your acquaintance. Pray remember my very kind respects to your good brother and sister [i.e. sister-in-law]. I hope to see you within this month. After the next Terme I shall be a little more at leisure. As often as I may serve you, pray let me heare from you, for I am to my power as zealous for you as any one in this Nation ... Thus hopeing to heare from you as often as you have occasion of my service, I wish you health and happiness and am, Good sir, your affectionate friend and servant,

Jo Aubrey. (Ballard 14, 80r)

This, the first of Aubrey's letters to Wood, is strikingly warm and enthusiastic; at first meeting Aubrey had recognised a kindred spirit whose single-minded devotion to the cause of antiquity he admired. Moreover, it shows how useful he could be to Wood; of the men on whom Wood asked for information, Serjeant Hoskyns was the grandfather of Aubrey's closest friend, and he knew John Owen's nephew and Digby's son, on whom he called two or three times 'in order to your Oxon. Antiqu' (B.L. Kenelme Digby).

Wood was to make ever more frequent demands on Aubrey over the next twenty-five years. On the insistence of Dr Fell, Dean of Christ Church, he was to include in his History notices of the more important writers and bishops educated at Oxford; after the History was published (1677), he later developed these short lives into *Athenae Oxonienses*, 'an exact History of all the Writers and Bishops educated at Oxford', a massive work including nearly 2,000 lives. And so the information he required from Aubrey was mostly biographical. He would send Aubrey lists of queries which became more and more peremptory, and Aubrey went to infinite trouble to give him accurate answers.

It is easy to underestimate Aubrey's achievement in carrying out this task in an age when there were few books of reference. He was very well read and even when separated from his books was often able to tell Wood where to look for answers to his queries on figures from the past. For contemporaries he relied first on information gathered from his wide circle of friends, for instance Edmund Wyld, Elias Ashmole and William Dugdale. His researches often involved visits to churches where there were memorial inscriptions which he conscientiously transcribed, or to relatives or descendants of the subject of his enquiry. He frequently wrote to acquaintances for information and roped in friends in distant counties to assist.

None of this was easy; when Wood needed information on Robert Herrick, Aubrey wanted to question a cousin of the poet: 'I have been at least 7 times at Mr Heyrick Stationer, whom at last when I found, he is the most morose and unmorall man that I met with: He cares not for Mr A. Wood, 'twill be no credit to his cosen to be named in his booke, he would not take paines to answer his Queries' (F39, 433; 5 September 1691). Letters remained unanswered; Aubrey had to write several times to get a reply from his cousin Henry Vaughan (the poet): 'I have sent 2, if not 3, letters to Olor Iscanus [the Swan of Usk], and he haz not been so civil as to answer me: he is ingeniose, but prowd and humorous' (F39, 400; 29 April 1690). Even close friends were not always as helpful as they might have been: 'Mr Hooke and Mr Halley are LAZIE and have not yet look't for the title of S.W. Astronomie. I am just now going to them again' (F39, 437; 8 November 1692). When he had gathered the information Wood required, he would send it to him in long discursive letters in which answers to queries were often interspersed with reflections on other matters. Nor was this the end of the matter, since Wood sometimes lost his answers and, to Aubrey's irritation, asked for the same information again.

Apart from a few hiatuses in later years, this process went on continuously until the year of Wood's death (1695). All this Aubrey did with the utmost good nature, neither expecting nor receiving any reward apart from the occasional 'token' (a token of love, i.e. a small sum of money), which Aubrey received with reluctant gratitude. When Wood wrote promising to send a 'token', Aubrey replied : 'I so much value the friendship and the good worke you are about, that you must not speake of requitall ... the next summer I hope to see you, and your good conversation will abundantly recompence me' (F39, 163; 27 January 1672).

Wood replied promptly to Aubrey's first letter with a warm and grateful answer, showing the value he put on his help:

Oxon, Jan.13,1668

Sir,

Yesterday I received yours dated Jan.8th with several papers and *Notitia Oxon* inclosed, for which I cannot but render you many thanks, coming at this time seasonably to my hands, being now about (if not hindred) Trinity Coll.: and for some other things which you promised me <that> will I hope come time enough. I wish I had acquaintance with more of your publick spirit who might certifie me concerning such matters ... Much more could I write unto you, but hoping for your company about a month hence, I shall forbeare till that time, when I may be further satisfied by word of mouth; in the mean time wishing you free from your troubles, I desire to kiss your hand and be esteemed, Sir, your most humble servant,

AW (Ballard 14, 80v)

Aubrey was back in Oxford a fortnight after he received this letter and spent the evening with Wood at the Crown Tavern, after which Wood paid the extravagant sum of 6d 'to Robert Prudhomme, Mr Aubrey's man, for lighting me home' (L & T ii, 126). He was there again the following May. His visits were becoming frequent and were always a joy and refreshment of spirit: 'As soon as my lawe suite will give me leave, I will lengthen my life a little by reviving my spirits at Oxon' (11 November 1668, Ballard 14, 82). After his visit he wrote again:

London May 19,1668

Mr Woodes!

(he will send info on both Hoskyns & Jo Owen. Long note on 'That sweet Swan of Isis Sr Wm Davenant, who dyed the seventeenth day of April last …')

I am beholding to you for remembering my great great grandfather Dr W Aubrey …

Pray present my humble service to Dr Bathurst and his ingeniose Lady. Mr Dugdale remembers him kindly to you and hath a great respect for you. I shall stay in Towne yet three weekes.

Your Affectionate friend and servant

J Aubrey

My kind respects and thankes to your good Brother for my good entertainment. (F39, 118)

Aubrey's great great grandfather William (1529–95) of Brecon was the one member of his family who had achieved distinction; he became Master of the Chancery and Vicar General to the Archbishop of Canterbury: 'Queen Elizabeth loved him and was wont to call him "her little Doctor"' (B.L. William Aubrey).

Aubrey wrote again in July sending Wood some papers via Bathurst:

Broad Chalke July 19 1668

Sir,

I sent a letter about May, which I hope came to your hands. I should be as glad to serve you to my power as any one in the world.

I am sorry I was so unfortunate to misse Dr Bathurst yesterday … I sent this by the Dr's servant, being unwilling to adventure it by the carrier [papers enclosed]

When you are pleased to lay your commands on me, direct your letter

to the Lamb in Katherine Street in Salisbury. Sir, I rest in hast (not yet having ended my lawe suite)
Your very affectionate friend and humble servant

Jo Aubrey

In December Wood asked Aubrey to help him get employment in the Heralds' Office, a post which would have suited his talents very well. Wood had met William Dugdale, at this time Chester Herald, the previous June, when he went to London for the first time to study the records in the Tower; Dugdale, one of the greatest scholars of his time, was working there on the third volume of his *Monasticon*, and looked after Wood, whose ability he came to respect. Aubrey knew Dugdale well and was prepared to act on Wood's behalf:

London Dec.5th, 1668

Mr Woodes!

I received your kinde letter and had sooner writ to you could I have met Mr Dugdale, who yesterday and this night very courteously remembers him to you and assures me he will be willingly ready to serve you, and the rather for that there is not any one so fitt for such employment as your selfe. There is not any vacancy yet, but he supposes one that I know that is not fitt for the place will be contented for money to resigne. He is Lancaster Herald and one that the office (and I thinke every body) hates, or ought to doe, if they knew him as well as I doe, for he was the *boute feu* [firebrand] to sett my dame and me at Variance. Mr Dugdale will try what is to be donne and doe what is possible. All lovers of this learning ought to rejoice when you shall be made an ornament in the office. (F39, 121)

The Lancaster Herald was Captain Robert Chaloner, appointed in the previous year; what part he played in the Joan Sumner affair, we do not know. Wood wrote promptly to thank Aubrey:

Oxon Dec.8th 1668

Good Mr Aubrey,

I am glad to have such a friend as you to stir in my business. I would by no means have put you to this trouble, could I have reposed confidence in any other. ... Pray, Sir, move once more in this business so far as I desire and you will ever engage me to be

your most humble servant, Ant. Wood. (F39, 121v)

Chaloner was not to be bought out; he held the office until he died in 1675. Wood's way was firmly blocked and he never got a post in the Heralds' office despite Aubrey's continued attempts to press the matter with Dugdale.

The letters show that relations between Wood and Aubrey were now very warm and that while Wood was coming to depend on Aubrey, the latter thoroughly enjoyed his company.

The following summer Wood had a furious quarrel with his sister-in-law which had consequences disastrous for him:

> June 26 (1669), AW was dismist from his usual and constant diet which for many yeares he had taken in the house where he was borne and then lived, by the rudeness and barbarity of a brutish woman, of which she afterwards repented, when too late. A.W. was put to his shifts, a great deale of trouble, and knew not what to do ... He was ashamed to go to a public house, because he was a senior master, and because his relations lived in Oxon: and to go to Merton Coll., he was much resolv'd in himself against it ... By his much fasting, and drinking more than usually, the whole course of his body was chang'd. Weakness came into severall of his joynts, especially in his leggs, and great noises in his eares; and in the next yeare he found a deafness, first in his right, and afterwards in his left, eare, which continued more or less till death. This disaster A.W. look'd upon as the first and greatest misery of his life. It made him exceedingly melancholy and retired; and was also at great charg in taking physick and slops, to drive the noises out of his eares. (L & T 11, 163–4)

He must have made this entry in his autobiography many years later, and the deterioration in his hearing and his general health must have been gradual. His diary shows him still enjoying convivial evenings with friends in the Mermaid and other taverns for the next few years. His health is not mentioned in the letters which passed between him and Aubrey until 1678, when he made his first visit to Bath to attempt a cure by taking the waters: 'June 29 (1678), I returned to Oxford from Bath, where I had been from 30 of May, but received no benefit' (L & T ii, 412). But no doubt he had to give up the music which had been one of the great joys of his life, and his increasing deafness must have been a perpetual worry and irritation and helps to account for the bad temper and quarrelsomeness which characterise his later years.

For the present there is no shadow over his relations with Aubrey. After a visit to Oxford in the summer of 1669, Aubrey wrote hoping to entertain him at Broad Chalke:

> Salisbury Aug.7, 1669
>
> Deare Friende!
>
> I returne my heartie respects and thankes to you for your great kinde-

nesses to me at Oxon, which I must never forgett: and without complement I never was more happy in any one's company in my life ...

I should be the happiest man to see you in Wilts. About ten dayes hence I shall know when I maye be certayne to be found. I have now but one horse fitt to be rid, els I would send one for you. I will send again to you shortly. In the interim I rest in Hast, Deare Anthony,

Your most affectionate and obliged friend and servant,

Jo Aubrey. (F39, 123)

In January of the following year he wrote to Wood:

Sarum St Paul's Day (25 January) 1670

Sir,

My kind respects remembered unto you. I heard lately that Mr Rogers Principall of New-Inne-Hall is dead, whereby that place I hope falls to your government....

Your booke I presume hath been a good while in the Presse.

I thinke about the end of Terme I may be at London ... I have the prospect of Osney severall other wayes then that in the Monasticon ... (Ballard 14, 86r)

This page and following: *A drawing from Aubrey's* Designato de Easton Piers *of the house where he was born, by kind permission of the Bodlein Library*

On several occasions both Aubrey and Wood had entertained vain hopes that they might be elected head of a college (see pages 71–2). When Aubrey was still an undergraduate at Trinity he had commissioned drawings of Osney Abbey which had been one of the greatest priories in England, partly demolished at the Dissolution and now about to be finally razed to the ground. He always considered this first attempt to save the past from 'the teeth of Time' highly significant. He had lent one of the drawings to Dugdale for his *Monasticon*, who had it engraved by Wenceslaus Hollar. Now he offered them to Wood for his History.

On 22 October (1669) Wood had been summoned by the Delegates of the university press and told that they would give him £100 for his manuscript of *The History and Antiquities of the University of Oxon*, 'conditionally that he would suffer the book to be translated into Latin'. Latin, the common language of educated men throughout Europe, had always been used for works of learning, but this was ceasing to be the custom; important works now often appeared in the vernacular (one of the last to be published in Latin was Newton's *Principia* (1686–7)). Wood accepted this offer, which was to cause him infinite trouble, since Dr Fell, Dean of Christchurch and the Vice-Chancellor, took charge of both the translation and publication and made numerous alterations in the text. Aubrey, who was to be deeply involved in the subsequent

controversy with Fell, wrote a letter to Wood the following February, in which he questioned the decision to publish the History in Latin: 'For if it is first in English, it will bring it into far more fame and sell the better.' (Ballard 14, 84; 17 February 1670)

Receiving no reply to this letter, he wrote to Wood again in April, his last letter from Easton Piers, which he had inherited from his grandfather and was now compelled by his financial straits to sell:

Easton Pierse, Easter Tuesday (= 5 April) 1670

Honest Mr Anthony,

I sent you a letter from London last terme, by the Coachman; I never heard from you since, and therefore suspect that he being drunk lost it. The content of it was to give you notice that if you have occasion of search and transcription of any records at Rome, I can have it donne for you. I am very well acquainted with the Provinciall of the Jesuits, who will send to their Generall at Rome, who hath promised it shall be donne, if you send me your Queres or proposalls ...

I shall thinke the time long till I enjoy your good company ... I am now takeing leave of this beloved place, where I first drew breathe. I have now lately ended my lawe-suite with Mris Sumner. I should be glad to see you in Wiltshire and to take a pilgrimage with you to Malmesburie.

If in any thing I may serve you, pray freely command me, being, Sir, your truly affectionate friend and humble servant, Jo Aubery.

My kind respects I pray to your brother and Mr Hine and also to Dr Bathurst. The next weeke I shall goe to Chalke, where I hope not to stay above 10 or 14 dayes; and then to London. This, that if occasion be, you may know how to send to me.

Vivas et valeas [Long life and good health]. (Tanner 456a, 9)

The sale of Easton Piers was completed in March 1671: 'Then [i.e. after the lawsuit with Joan Sumner] sold Easton-Pierse ... lost 500 li + 200 li + goods + timber. Absconded as a banish'd man' (Auto).

Neither the sale of Easton Piers nor the conclusion of his lawsuit with Joan Sumner brought Aubrey any relief. He now had no security against his debts and could see no way of ever paying off his creditors: 'I was in as much affliction as a mortall could bee, and was never quiet till all was gone, (and I) wholly cast myselfe on God's providence' (Auto). For the rest of his life he was almost always in danger of arrest for debt and frequently had to go into hiding to avoid the 'catch polls'. And yet his reaction to this situation was not despair but relief, as if he had rid himself of a heavy burden:

I had never quiett, nor anything of happinesse till divested of all, 1670,1671: at what time providence raysed me (unexpectedly) good friends – the right honourable Nicholas, earl of Thanet, with whom I was

> delitescent at Hethfield in Kent neer a yeare [see Chapter 5]; ... Sir Christopher Wren, Mr Ogilby [see Chapter 5]; then Edmund Wyld esq, Fellow of the Royal Society of Glasely Hall, Salop tooke me into his armes, with whom I most commonly take my diet and sweet otiums. (Auto)

Wyld was a wealthy and hospitable friend with whom Aubrey continually sat up late drinking; he was a great raconteur and supplied Aubrey with a lot of material of *Brief Lives.*

The autobiographical notes go no further than about 1680 and one might add others who took him in their arms in later years, above all his cousin Sir John Aubrey of Llanthrydid, Dr William Holder, rector of Therfield in Hertfordshire, James Bertie, Earl of Abingdon; Aubrey never lacked good friends who were glad to have him to stay with them for long periods.

Chapter IV

Aubrey Absconds 1670–71

FAR FROM SINKING INTO LETHARGY under the weight of his affliction, Aubrey worked with a new sense of urgency:

> Anno 1671, having sold all and disappointed of moneys I received, I had so strong an impulse to (in good part) finish my *Description of Wilts*, two volumes in folio, that I could not be quiet till I had donne it, and that with danger enough, *tamquam canis e Nilo* [like a dog escaping from the Nile], for feare of the crocodiles, i.e. catch-polls. (Auto)

Nevertheless, the prospect must have seemed desperate and he considered two possible ways of escaping from his intolerable situation. The first was to turn Catholic and enter a monastery: 'I wished monastrys had not been putt downe, that the reformers would have been more moderate as to that point ... fitt there should be receptacles and provision for contemplative men' (Auto). The second was to emigrate to the plantations, a recurring theme in the letters over the years, as he was repeatedly offered openings by well-wishers.

In November 1670 he wrote to Wood from Broad Chalke. He had already 'absconded' and was hiding from his creditors and had to travel 'invisibly'. After answering a long list of Wood's queries, he reports the progress he has made on the *Wiltshire Antiquities* and the work he has done on Roman camps and roads, which was to form Part 2 of *Monumenta Britannica*, and on natural history, which was later to be incorporated into the Preface to the *Natural History of Wiltshire*:

> Broadchalke Nov.17,1670
>
> Deare Mr Woods!
>
> I thinke I have now donne about 3 parts of 4 of Wilts. I hope next spring in a fortnight or 3 weeks to doe (invisibly) the remaynder. I know not how or why, methinkes, but I have a kind of divine impulse to have it donne; no body els will doe it and when 'tis donne, none in these parts will value it, but the next generation I hope will be less brutish.
>
> I have a quire of Chorographia Antiquaria and a map and discourse upon it, viz. the Roman and British and Danish camps – highways, and traced Offa's dyke from Severne to Dee and Wednesdyke, and rectified Mr Camden [i.e. corrected Camden's *Britannia*] in some places, and pretend

[= claim] to tell where Boudicca's battle was. Nothing is in it yet (except some eminent ways) that hath been donne already. I have surveied the camps; found out the places of the battles by the barrows. Mr Hoskyns and Dr Ball saye it is the best thing I have donne, but 'tis drie meate.

Between South Wales and the French sea I have taken an account of the severall earths and naturall observables in it, and the nature of plants in the respective soyles, the nature of the cattle thereon feeding, and the nature of the Indigenae [the natives] ...

I will write other things next time, being now weary,

Tuissimus, J.A. (F39, 128)

It is not surprising that he was weary, but he follows this account with a characteristic P.S. almost as long as the preceeding letter, in which he muses on his situation and for the first time considers the alternative plans of emigrating to the plantations or taking refuge in a monastery:

I desire to have the Nativity which you told me you would looke out. See the Preface of Mr Gadbury's Almanac 1671; His proposals for the Advancement of Astrology: I can furnish him with an excellent and exact copie and that of men of note in severall waies. But the Deane of Wells [Ralph Bathurst] would laugh at this, but Kepler and Tycho Brahe would not ...

Consider, were you in my case, whether you would choose the advantage I may make in Maryland (but *cui bono*? [for whose good?]) or IHS (the Society of Jesus)? ... We have amongst us so much Saving Faith, that justice and charity are out of fashion ... but your Genevists etc are as superstitious as the Romans, but doe not know it ...

I doe thinke it might be sayd of Antiquaries as of Poets, *nascuntur, non fiunt* [they are born, not made], and also beleeve that you are driven by the same impulse for your worke. I would faine methinkes doe some good in the world if I could before I dye: *ne videar inutilis esse servus* [lest I should seem to be a useless servant].

Aubrey asks Wood to send him his Nativity. At this time he had become deeply interested in astrology, seeing in the influence of the planets an explanation of the many troubles which beset him. He hoped to contribute to the 'science' of astrology by making a collection of accurate nativities of distinguished men, a project on which he worked for many years. He repeatedly asked Wood for his nativity in more and more urgent terms: 'I doe require and enjoyne you by the sacred friendship between us, that you send me exactly the yeare, day and hower, if possible, when you were borne, and where, which will be of great use for the Advancment of Astrology; I have and shall gett 30 Nativities exactly; many of them of men famous in Learning, Wealth, Valour etc.' (F39, 131, 14 June 1671). But Wood did not oblige him, being a sceptic in such matters.

Aubrey had been offered a post in Maryland by Lord Baltimore, whose brother was Governor. As for turning Catholic, Aubrey had little use for Puritans of any complexion and was, as he says in a later letter, no enemy to Roman Catholics, 'unless they be Irish bigots'. His own attitude to religion was tolerant and rationalistic; he objected more to the intolerance and hypocrisy of the Puritans than to the 'superstition' of the Roman Church and may have been seriously tempted to convert to Rome and take refuge in a monastery.

In his Accidents Aubrey says of 1671 'Danger of arrests', and he spent much time avoiding the 'catch-polls' or 'mewed up' at Broad Chalke. When he did travel, he was incognito; so when he wanted to visit Wood at the end of the year before emigrating, he says: 'I have a desire to see you once or twice more and I cannot have a more clowdy opportunity for an invisible ghost than now' (F39, 149; 20 December 1671). In August he wrote from Chalke sending Wood several pages of miscellaneous information and thanking him for promising to make an honourable mention of him in his book: 'I wish I were as able as willing to serve you ... I am much beholding to you for the honour that you are pleased to let my name live. Pray putt in my beloved Easton Pierse where, and to which estate, I was borne: if Heaven had pleased, I might still have enjoyd it' (F39, 135; 9 August, 1671). Wood did indeed make a single mention of Aubrey, acknowledging that he had sent him an epitaph, but this was a poor reward for all the work Aubrey had done for him.

Later in the month Aubrey was staying with Hoskyns at Harewood, a few miles south of Hereford, from where he wrote sending Wood information on Oxford worthies buried in the cathedral. On his return to Broad Chalke, he received the following answer from Wood:

Sept.23,1671

Deare Sir,

I have received your letter dated Hereford Sept 2, for which I heartily thank you and those things therein, which stand me in good stead ...

You desired me also that Mr Hine should not know where you were; I shall not tell him; however asking him the other day at his arrival from his own country of Somersetshire, I asked him where you were: he told me you were turned priest and were gone to France to enter yourself into a Monasterie, which was the vogue of all the people at Kington and thereabout: I have heard this from severall people, particularly from the family of the Dean of Wells [Bathurst] ...Tell me your mind as to this, and I shall be as secret in it as a confessor.

I sent you a letter dated Aug 22 containing many queries. My booke goes on as yet slowly but will I hope <go> faster to my content; God

send me happy deliverance of it, it will bee 200 sheets and full of cuts [illustrations], so the price may be 40s if not 50s.
Yrs, yrs, yrs, AW (Tanner 456a, 12)

Richard Hine was a Fellow of Merton and a friend of Wood; he was a Wiltshire man, long known to Aubrey. But his father was the attorney employed by Joan Sumner, and Aubrey was most anxious that he should not know his whereabouts. He replied to Wood with what is perhaps the longest of his surviving letters (six folios closely written on both sides), in which he gives answers to Wood's queries interspersed with reflections on his present position and future and plans:

Broad Chalke Oct 27,1671

My Worthy Friend,

I returned hither this day 3 weeks, and am very much to blame I have not answered your 2 kind letters Aug.22 and Sept.23 sooner ...

I am mightely pleasd to have it confirmed so certainely that I am beyond the sea: at Salisbury 'tis for certain that I am in Italy, let it be Bononia (Bologna): these things I have given out for my owne security; but 'tis perhaps prophetically true. After so many tossings and troubles in the world, where could a man better withdraw him selfe then into such a learned Society as IHS (study they must; but what they have a mind to: musick, Heraldry, chymistry etc.). I am well acquainted with one and always reserved that designe as the *ultimum refugium* [last refuge]. To goe to reconcile the differences of the two churches I leave to them which have nothing else to doe and know not how to spend their paines better. This is certayne to my knowledge, and everyone that hath been amongst 'em, that no vertuous person shall want, and for promoting of any publique businesse, they will fly and turne every stone. Now amongst others I correspond with is Father Thimelby (bro to Sr Th. Thimelby of Yorkshire), who is now rector of a pretty little college of Novices in a pleasant place (Watton) 6 miles from Dunkirke, who hath invited me over to him above this 12 moneth and stay as long as I will sojourne. And after 40, what better life could a man take? ... Prithee, Mr Woods, tell Dr. Bathurst and his godly Lady that you have received a letter from Bononia and that I am in Heaven upon earth. Tell 'em fryar John remembers him to them: as also to Mr Hine, and that difference in Religion should not breed difference in affection etc.

Now I come (as Dr Kettle would say) to the purpose. Before I went to Herefordshire I writt to my old acquaintance the Bishop of Sarum [Seth Ward] to send to Exeter for Sr Walter Rawlegh's Epitaph with some other Quaeries, which he could command, among others Bishop Jewell's Epitaph at Sarum, which my brother [Tom] will write out to morrow. I writt to his Lordship as upon the publiq account for your booke, with great apologising etc, yet I did not expect that a person of his greatness should write himselfe about these matters, but tell his secretary, chaplaine or etc of it: *Fac hoc, et facit* ['Do this, and he doeth it', Luke 7, 8]. The Devill an answer I received: he scornes it. I'm confident never a one of the Cardinalls would have served me thus; I have therefore sent to one in Devonshire for all such quaeries, as also in Cornwall, particularly for Sidney Godolphin's obiit etc, which I dayly expect.

I would willingly, before I leave England, finish my perambulation of Wilts, which is more than half donne. In a fortnight or 3 weeks I could doe the Country part. The records will keepe cold. I thinke I must leave the finishing to you or Mr Browne: but rather you, when you are at leisure; about March or April I hope to finish as afore sayd, and leave it with you …

I have severall mundane businesses first to dispatch. I heartily wish I were at Wotton with Father Thimelby for a quarter or half yeare; no life would like me better. For *cui bono* [for whose good?] should I now make my selfe a slave to bee rich? Riches and honours etc are fine things for 25 or 30, but I vowe to God I would not be Bishop of Sarum for the trouble on't. I was left 600li per annum, or better, my mother and I together: and I should have been glad to have kept it, or at least turnd it to my brothers. But never was man so plagued with an Estate. I have now these 3 weekes more enjoyed my selfe than I have in the 19 yeares since my father dyed. I am writing of a comedy for Thomas Shadwell (dramatist, poet, theatrical entrepreneur), which I have almost finished since I came home *et quorum pars magna fui* ['in which I have played a great part' Virgil Aeneid ii, 6], and I shall fitt him with another, *The Country Revell*; both humours untoucht [i.e. original], which I in my tumbling up and downe have collected; but of this Mum, for 'tis satiricall against some of my mischievous enemies.

Now if I would be rich, I could be a prince. I could goe to Maryland (between Virginia and New England), which is one of the finest countrys of the world (same climate with France). I can have all the favour of Lord Baltimore I could wish. His brother is his Lieutenant there, and a very good natured gent. Plenty of all things; there is ground 2000 miles westward. I could be able, I believe, to carry a colony of rogues, another of ingenious Artificers, and I doubt not but one might make a shift to have 5 or 6 ingeniose companions, which is enough.

Now which of these I shall choose *dabitur illa hora* ['will be given at that hour', i.e. 'time will reveal'], but of both these I adjure you by the friendship you beare me to be Secret …

I writt long since to Easton Pierse to my brother William to send you my Booke B (the second Book of the *Wiltshire Antiquities*), which I hope you have. I have ὕλη [material] enough to fill up ten leaves there at least; be pleased to blott out there some things wanton, and putt in what you thinke fitt, and when you have donne, send it hither …

I wish I were as able as willing to serve you. I am sorry to see that amongst a great many spiritual persons, I find so great a scarcity of Publiq Spirit …

Mr Hobbes told me that if he thought Magdalen Hall would accept friendly of it, he would give them his workes; which let them know by Mr Browne ... I heartily wish my selfe with you for 2 or 3 dayes, but it will be towards March 1st; I intend to see you before I go beyond the sea ... When you write, remember to endorse your letter to Mr Thomas Aubrey at Broad Chalk, to be left at the Lambe in Katherine Street, Sarum, to avoyd my being discovered.

Now I desire you to pardon my tediousness and to believe that I am with all my heart

Your very affectionate and humble servant,

Jo Aubrey.

Direct your letter thus: to Mr William Aubrey at Mr Stokes House in Kington St Michael. The carrier goes by it.

I was informed in Hereford by a learned man and one worthy of beleef that there is a Fellow of your house can conjure and one that has quieted howses that have been troubled. For God's sake let me know. I should be glad to be acquainted with him. (F39, 141)

Aubrey appears in this letter to have made up his mind that he must leave England, either for a monastery or for the plantations. In the meantime he was thoroughly enjoying his forced retirement, which gave him a little peace; his resilience now and throughout the rest of his life is truly astonishing. He can laugh at his situation and relishes the thought of Wood giving Bathurst a message from 'Fryar John.' He is deeply wounded at having received no reply from Seth Ward and supposes he has become too grand to bother with him (wrongly, as it happened; Ward did answer his query later). Nothing remains of the first comedy Aubrey refers to but fragments of *The Country Revel* lie scattered in his miscellaneous papers, enough to show that it was typical of Restoration comedy with characters such as Sir Fastidious Overween, Captain Exceptious Quarrellsome etc. and that its theme was an attack on contemporary manners compared with those of the good old days.

Richard Browne was a student of Magdalen Hall (later Hertford College), who sometimes did research for both Wood and Aubrey. Of Aubrey's brothers, Tom was running the farm at Broad Chalke, William was living as a lodger with Mr Stokes at Kington Manor, near Easton Piers. Aubrey enrolled them both from time to time to help with his researches. Wood must have been puzzled to know which address he should use.

Wood replied the very morning he received this letter, while the carrier waited:

Nov.10th, 1671

Deare Sir,

I received your large letter at 10 this morning, and because Ric Pope a carrier goes from Oxon this afternoon towards your parts, I thought to give you this short answer for the present.

I am verie glad that you have satisfied me in so many things and cease not to send into diverse parts for further information of other men: I speake in my conscience (for I have told other men of it already) that I have had and shall have more from you as to those things than all people besides whatsoever. What I have had hitherto besides hath been, for the most part, by mine owne industry and purse.

I am sorry there is so bad an understanding between you and the Bishop [Seth Ward]. I am confident that 'tis not on your part, but rather his; he is sickly and peevish, as I heare, and Salisbury aire doth so ill agree with him, that he is going to live at Lavington. If the Epitaph of Sir Walt. Rawlegh cannot be gotten with ease, let it rest, but 'tis pity such an opportunity of remembering so worthy a person should for want of so small a labour be omitted.

The report goes on here still of your being beyond the seas and that you are reconciled to the Church of Rome, which being pleasing to you, is to me also. The truth is, nothing is more delightfull to me then retiredness, and were I in your condition, I should take the same course that you have or are like to doe. I doe alwaies think of those words *omnia vanitas* ['all is vanity']; and *cui bono* [for whose good?] do we keep a clutter in this foolish world? methinkes scholars and contemplative men should look upon it and the things therein as below them. There be but three things that I strive to follow: these are: 1. To be above the desire of riches. 2. above the feare of death. 3. To be mine owne Judge and not be led away by what is put into my head by every person. Pray consider these things and obtain them and Ile warrant you a true philospher. I shall tell Dr Bathurst and his Lady what you desire. I know they will laugh at it …

I thinke no person fitter then my selfe to keep your Collections in case you leave us: if Mr Browne will doe any thing to them (the which I believe he cannot, because call'd away to other studies in order to a livelihood), he shall have them … He is certainly a hopefull man and 'tis pity that no encouragement is shew'd to him. I am resolveed to put him upon standing for a fellowship in our house next yeare; Ile do all my endeavours to get him as many votes as I can …

I have read your Book B [i.e. Book 2 of the *Wiltshire Collections*] and have almost done him; if you have any more to follow, I would gladly see them. I read these Collections with great delight and have excerpted some things there for my purpose …

I know none of our house that can conjure; there are not such profound men. Pray God they meane not me, for I have had that put upon me by

fools and asses – the Carrier staies and you shall heare more from me by the next. In the meantime I am your most humble servant,
AW

for Mr Thomas Aubrey of Broad Chalke. Pd.2d (A13, 263)

In this letter we see Wood at his best. He generously acknowledges the help he has received from Aubrey. He sympathises with his predicament. If his philosophy sounds complacent, it is only fair to say that he did live up to his three principles, even when the third threatened trouble. He is fair to young Richard Browne and determined to help him. He praises Aubrey's Book B, which he has read with great delight. The possibility that it was he who was said to be the 'conjurer' of Merton, dismays him; because he was eccentric by the standards of the day, he was making enemies, whose commonest accusation was that he was a crypto-Catholic. This rumour became increasingly prevalent since he had made the acquaintance of the prominent Catholic antiquarian Ralph Sheldon of Weston Park. Sheldon had met Wood in Oxford:

July 21, 1671 ... Mr Sheldon told AW that he had a great love for the study of antiquity, and that if he had any occasion for a cut (i.e. illustration), or cuts, to put in his book, he would freely give him one or more. This was the beginning of the acquaintance between Mr Sheldon and AW. And seeing that he sought after him and desired his acquaintance, he could not in civilitie denie him etc. Now Mr Sheldon being a zealous Papist, and AW afterwards being often in his company, must be esteem'd a Papist also, as he was by many of the sniveling saints, who make it a most horrible thing to be seen in the company of any one of them. (L & T, ii, 228)

Wood, a staunch royalist, had a hearty contempt for Puritans of every colour, but he was never a Catholic. These rumours and the increasing hostility he experienced were among the causes of his later embitterment.

Aubrey had long known Sheldon and in a letter of the following February he passes on to Wood an invitation to stay at Weston, which was to be the first of his many and ever longer visits there:

London, Feb 1 1672

Mr Woods,

I sent a letter lately to you to acquaint you that I am leaving this Towne, which I shall [do] God willing Satterday or Munday next, and then if I may farther serve you be pleased to direct your letter – To be left with Will. Darvell neer the Markett house in Wells.

Mr Sheldon of Weston (about twenty miles from Oxon) hath a very good collection of MSS and hath all the bookes of Heraldry etc., viz. the library of Mr Vincent the Herald.

He is a most candid, worthy gent, and with whom I have been long acquainted; and he would have you come to him the next summer, after June, where you shall be very welcome; and I will come along with you, if I can.

Dr Chris Wren hath putt a trick on us as it seems, for he hath made himself a yeare younger then indeed he is, though he needs not to be ashamed of his age: he hath made such admirable use of his time ...

Vale JA (F39, 165)

Aubrey continued to answer Wood's endless queries. A letter of January (1672) includes an account of Judge David Jenkins, who had married the sister of Aubrey's cousin Sir John Aubrey; this is worth quoting at length, both for its own sake and because it was to become one of the causes of the great quarrel with Wood:

London Jan.16,1672

Mr Wood,

I sent a letter to you about a fortnight ago ... David Jenkins (judge) was borne at Henlas ...He was one of the Judges of the Camarthen, Cardigan and Pembrokeshire Circuit before the wars. In the Warres he was taken prisoner at Hereford. Long time prisoner in the Tower, Newgate, Wallingford, and Windsore. Never submitted to the Usurping power (I think he was the onlie man). All his Estate was confiscated: and he was always excepted by the Parliament in the first rank of delinquents. In his circuit in Wales at the beginning of the Warres, he caused to be indicted severall men of these parts (that were parliament etc engaged against the King) for High Treason, and the grand Jury indicted them: afterwards when he was a prisoner in Newgate, some of these Grandees came to him to triumph over him, and told him that if they had been thus in his power, he would have hanged them: 'God forbid els,' replied he: which undaunted returne they much admired. The Parliament intended to have hanged him, and he expected no lesse, but resolved to be hanged with the Bible under one arme and Magna Carta under the other; and hanged he had been, had not Harry Martyn told them in the House, that *Sanguis Martyris est Semen Ecclesiae* [The blood of a martyr is the seed of the Church]; and that way they would doe them the more mischief. So his life was spared, and they removed him out of the way to Wallingford Castle ...'Twas pity he was not made one of the Judges of Westminster Hall for his long suffering, and he might have been (he told me) if he would have given money to the Chancellor; but he scorned it. (F39, 160)

Twenty years later, when Wood came to write an account of Judge

Jenkins in *Athenae Oxonienses*, he repeated much of Aubrey's letter verbatim, including the libel on the Chancellor, Clarendon, whose son brought an action against him for *Scandalum Magnatum*.

A month later, still at Broad Chalke, Aubrey wrote with answers to a new batch of Wood's queries, including information on his cousin Henry Vaughan, the poet:

Broad Chalk March 14,1672

Mr Woods,

Tomorrow I am going towards Somerset ... There were two Vaughans (Twinnes), both very ingeniose, and writers; one writt a Poem called *Olor Iscanus* [The Swan of Usk] (Henry, the first borne) and another a book of divine meditations ...They were borne at Llanscanfrid in Brecknockshire upon the River Uske. Their grandmother was an Aubrey, their father a coxcombe, and no honester then he should be; he cousened me of 50li. once ...

You must needs go to Mr Sheldon, who will make you very kindly welcome.

Vivas et valeas [long life and good health!],

Tuissimus (your dearest friend), Jo. Albericus

This is the first mention in Aubrey's extant letters of his cousins the Vaughans; Henry and his twin brother Thomas had both been at Jesus College, Oxford. Henry returned to Brecknockshire, where he practised medicine, writing his great poetry in his spare time. Aubrey carried on a correspondence with him on subjects such as astrology, Welsh bards, and natural history. Thomas, a divine and an alchemist, had died in 1666.

There follows a P.S. which contains two folios of answers to queries. Wood had asked for the epitaph of the Elizabethan poet Samuel Daniel; Aubrey asked his brother William to send it: 'If my brother should not send you, which I hope he will, S. Danyels ISS, let the Deane of Wells send at his proper cost: he hath been a poet himself in his day. Prithee Anthony discourse with her Holiness a little about me ...I am now in Flaunders: I writt so to Mr Gore' (F39, 369). Bathurst had recently been appointed Dean of Wells and Aubrey, afraid that he may be 'inflated by his titles', often refers to him now as 'the Dean'. His wife was a sanctimonious woman for whom Aubrey had a hearty dislike.

Aubrey eventually got off to Somerset, to visit a cousin at Wells and perhaps to say goodbye to his mother, who was living at Bridgwater. From there he returned to Broad Chalke before setting off again to stay with Hoskyns at Harewood. Back at Broad Chalke he wrote to Wood:

Broad Chalke April 1st 1672

Dear Mr Woods,

I writt a long letter to you about the middle of March, which I left here to be sent with care; but my brother carryed it to Sarum and meeting with company forgott it and brought it back again. Which I found here at my returne from Wells and shall send it tomorrow with this. You sent a letter to me to Wells, which my cosen haz lost. On Satterday next (or Fryday) I shall be God willing at Harewood with Mr Hoskyns in Herefordshire, wher I shall stay about a moneth ...

I long to see you for one whole day, with the longing of a woman: were I more at liberty, I could serve you more: now I have halfe donne Wilts, 'tis pitty (me thinkes) but I should goe through with it, for I know nobody els would do it throughly like an Antiquary ...

I have no more at present but I am your truly affectionate friend to serve you,

JA (Ballard 14, 92r)

In May he fulfilled his longing to visit Wood and the visit seems to have been an unqualified success:

Broad Chalk, May 10,1672

Mr Wood!

I am so much obliged to you for your extreme kindness to me last week and your great charges, that I am not orator enough to expresse my thankfulnesse, but your candour will accept of a gratefull heart. I forgott to tell you that I shall take the invitation of a delitescence in Kent for some time. Thinke how I may serve you there. About the beginning of next weeke, I shall be in London, where I shall stay but a weeke ... 1000 thankes to you, so at 11 o'clock at night or past, I rest

Tuissimus, JA (F39, 171)

Chapter V

A Happy Delitescene 1672–73

THE DELITESCENCE IN KENT had been offered to Aubrey by Nicholas Tufton, Earl of Thanet, whose seat was at Hethfield near Ashford in Kent. An ardent royalist, twice imprisoned in the Tower during the Commonwealth, he was pedantic, censorious and self-opinionated, but he had a heart of gold and was one of Aubrey's principal benefactors until his early death in 1679. He had written to Aubrey in January (1672), offering him a refuge and a nominal job.

Although Aubrey had now decided to take up Thanet's offer, he was in no hurry to do so. He seems to have had a frantic itch to travel this year, despite the difficulties of maintaining his incognito. In May he wrote to Wood: 'On Monday, God willing, I goe into Essex, and life being short and uncertaine determine to goe thence to Norfolk, Suffolk, Cambridge, and so to London in about 10 dayes' (F39, 173, 25 May 1672). There is a certain hecticness about this tour, as if he really were bidding goodbye to his friends before going overseas.

Returning to London from his tour, in the course of which he had stayed with Sir Thomas Browne (*Religio Medici* etc.), he wrote briefly to Wood, enclosing answers to queries:

London June 18 1672

Mr Woods!

I received yours without date Sunday last. Have you the Epitaph etc of Bp Corbett, who is buried in Norwich but Inscription lost? If you have it not, Sr Th.Browne shall gett it. He received me with much humanity ...
(Answers to Queries)
A fortnight hence I am invited by a noble Earle into Kent, where I shall stay till Michaelmas and shall there serve you to my power. Direct yours to Mr H.Coley ...
in hast I rest

yrs JA (F39, 175r)

Henry Coley was an atrologer whom Aubrey much admired and with whom he frequently stayed at his house in Westminster. 'His fame increases every day, he is far from mountebanking as others are' (F39, 214).

Aubrey continued to delay his departure for Kent and in a letter to Wood explained that he had been detained by a new project:

London Aug.12,1672

Mr Woods!

I have not heard of you a pretty while: you supposed by this time I was gone to Kent, whither, God willing, I shall goe on Wednesday or Saterday ...

I had gone sooner into Kent but Dr Wren, my deare friend, without my knowledge contrived an employment for me, which he referred to me to consider of, and so I shall till Michaelmas Terme. 'Tis this: Mr Ogilby is writing a History of all England; the map is mending [i.e. is being improved] already. Now the Doctor (Wren) told him that if that were all, it would be no very great matter; he was pleased to tell him that he could not meet a fitter man for that turne then I. Now it's true it suites well enough with my Genius: but he [Ogilby] is a cunning Scott, and I must deale warily with him with the advise of my friends. It will be February next before I begin and then between that and November following I must curry over all England and Wales. I have severall good topiqs of Queries, but by my acquaintance I can have a stock of Queries sufficient by that time, and I shall not be wanting to thinke of A.W. The King will give me a protection and letters to make inquisition etc ...

You may remember me to Father Hine because my being in Towne is too much knowne, but tell him I am goeing toward France, which is true, for I am goeing to the sea-coast of Kent. Perhaps I may make a step to Calais (but tother side). I shall write to this purpose to my stiffe starcht friend T.G. Cuckold Esq. My service to the Deane and his good Lady.

This is all at present from

Yrs JA (F39, 181)

John Ogilby (1600–1676) had a remarkable career; starting as a dancing master, he had become an author and printer, was now 'King's Cosmographer' and was commissioned to make a new survey of all England and Wales. For this project he needed assistants and Wren had recommended Aubrey, to whom it particularly appealed since he would have protection from arrest while so employed. He had several meetings with Ogilby, Wren, Hooke and Hoskyns to discuss what this 'history' should include; a list of topics was drawn up and circulated by Ogilby: 'Queries in order to the Description of Britannia'. The list included houses of the nobility and gentry, sites of battles, waters, springs and baths, mines of metals and minerals, extraordinary accidents, calamities, and casualties etc. This was clearly conceived as a major project which would have occupied Aubrey for many years. But Ogilby's attitude was from the start ambivalent; he wanted his book in the press by November 1673 and may never have intended more than a new map of Britain, whereas Aubrey, Wren and Hooke had something very different in mind.

'My stiffe starcht friend T.G. Cuckold Esq.' is Thomas Gore, a disagreeable man who lived near Easton Piers; he had plagiarised some work of Aubrey on heraldry for which he had made no acknowledgement; as Aubrey wrote to Wood: 'he hath perused my MSS and donne his businesse, and now a fart for me'.

Just before he left for Hethfield Aubrey wrote a note to Wood promising to 'do his business in Kent'. In a P.S. he adds: 'I am glad your booke goes on so fast; I thanke for the honour you doe me in making my name live in your liveing Worke, to remayne for ever there like an unprofitable elder or yew tree on some noble structure' (F39, 183; 19 August 1672).

Aubrey left for Hethfield on 19 August (1672) and, keeping his promise to Wood, within three days of his arrival there wrote sending information, some of which he had gleaned from parish churches in Kent (F39, 185; 22 August 1672) and again on 6 September four pages of answers to queries (F39, 188). He seems to have been well content in his 'monastery' at Hethfield, and was in high spirits when he wrote to Wood in October:

> Hethfield Oct 22, 1672
>
> The wayes are so bad and aire so ill I stir not out of doors, but divert my selfe very pleasantly with algebra.
>
> (Answers to queries)
>
> When your booke is printed, then hey for Oxfordshire. I have the Prospect of Woodstock House and Parke …
>
> Have you seen Sr T. Browne's booke on Urne-Buriall? which he is now augmenting. I will bring you about March my other draughts of Osney ruines.
>
> I wish you had some more such impertinent scobberlotching (Dr Kettle) agents that wish as well to carrying on such publiq workes as these, as I doe. I thanke you for giving me that prudential caution of Mr Ogilby.
>
> I am in hast.
>
> Tuissimus JA
>
> (F39, 196, 22 October 1672)

'Hey for Oxfordshire': Wood planned to write an account of the antiquities of Oxfordshire when he had finished his history of the university.

Clearly, the bad weather had not dampened Aubrey's spirits; he was happy enough and, as his next letter shows, had time to reflect on matters other than his own immediate concerns:

I have a great desire to see my honest brother Tom well settled, i.e. marryed to a good discreet wife with about 800li or 1000, which his estate (Chalke Farm 250li per annum) doth very well deserve. I would you would find another as your sister-in-lawe, or neice is, if she were big enough; my great grandmother was of Oxfordshire and I like the people very well; about Chalke are no wives neerer than Salisbury, prowd and all gamesters and unknowing and unfitt for a country gent's turne; and in North Wilts they will be drunke. Is it not an odd thing to send to a monke and antiquary about such a query? But how can I tell what may happen. Some of your acquaintance may hint I intend to be at London about next Christmas. I have not enjoyed my selfe so much for 20 yeares as here ... About the latter end of February or all of March I am for Wool-gathering [i.e. travelling]. Thus with my hearty well-wishes for you, I rest,

Your most affectionate friend and servant,

Jo Aubrey (F39, 179; 28 November 1672)

Aubrey was back in London two days after writing this letter; Hooke records in his diary: 'Dec.1st: Mr Aubery first out of Kent.' (This diary runs from August 1672 until 1693, with some breaks, and is an invaluable source of information on Aubrey's movements).

From London Aubrey wrote to Wood, telling him of a new job his friends in the Royal Society had found for him:

London, Jan.1673

Deare Friend,

I have given to the Library of the Royal Society (among other good books) a manuscript of about <the time of> Henry 4, *scilicet Historia Roffensia*, which they will exchange with you at Oxon for some Mathematicall or Philosophicall bookes, for that they will have no bookes there but of those 2 sorts ...
Yours JA

The Royal Society have been pleased to lay their commands upon me to keepe a Correspondence with my numerous company of ingeniose Virtuosi in severall counties and will pay the expenses of Letters and will allow me something of an Honorarium besides. This intelligence is for things naturall or artificial or any thing remarqueable in philosophy or mathematiques. (F39, 253)

He must have been delighted by the commission to act as the Royal Society's correspondent. He was ideally suited for this task which he continued to perform for many years, corresponding on behalf of the Society not only with Virtuosi in England but also with friends who were overseas, especially on the natural history of the parts where they were living. Many of the answers he received are preserved in his collection of letters.

While in London, Aubrey wrote to Wood: 'I hope to retrive J. Dee's papers in Kent. Sir Thomas Browne told me where they are lodged' (F39, 181). John Dee, the great Elizabethan mathematician, alchemist and astrologer, had been a friend of his great-great-grandfather and Aubrey planned to write his life. He failed to find anything in Kent but his inquiries led him to make a cold trek into Surrey in December to Mortlake, where Dee had lived in his old age, as he told Wood:

> Last month I went on a pilgrimage 5 miles in the frost afoote to search the register at Mortlack in Surrey; '*hic etiam non inventus est J.Dee*' [even here I did not find J.Dee]. I was then directed to inquire of old goody Faldo, *aetat* [aged] 80, and yet a lusty woman. She knew Dr Dee, and her mother tended him in his sicknesse, and she exactly told me the place where he lyes buryed in that church of Mortlack. (F39, 192, 18 January 1673)

'Old goody Faldo' proved remarkably informative considering her great age: 'She sayd, he kept a great many Stilles goeing [for his experiments in alchemy]. That he layd the storme. That the children dreaded him because he was accounted a Conjuror …' (B.L. Dee) He sent an account of what he had learnt to Elias Ashmole, the founder of the Ashmolean Museum, an old friend expert in alchemy and astrology; Ashmole visited Mortlake himself the following August and eventually recovered Dee's papers.

Four days later he wrote again to say that he was about to return to Hethfield:

> London Jan 22 1673
>
> Mr Wood!
>
> [JA is continuing his inquiries]
>
> On Wednesday I am for Kent. My Lord haz sent for me again, and tomorrow night a horse will be brought for me: I shall then and there not be unmindfull of your other Q. I am just now goeing to our worthy good friend Mr Elias Ashmoll.
>
> I dyned yesterday with my ever honoured friend Dr Ch Wren, who much commends him to you.
>
> Pray do not forget in Oxford honest friendly H. Coley …
>
> For God's sake (if possible) retrive your Nativity.
>
> Thus wishing you well, I rest in hast,
>
> yours JA (F39, 195)

Wood must have written to Aubrey complaining of the alterations and additions which Dr Fell had made to his History while it was in the press. This caused Wood great distress and led to a bitter controversy between him and Fell in which Aubrey took a leading part. Aubrey, still in London, replied on 3 February:

London Feb.3 1673

Deare AW!

I received yours of the Conversion of St Paul [= 25 January], for which I returne heartie thankes. I am truly sorry for the Foystings so disingenuously imposed to blemish the best worke that was ever yet donne in that nature. I acquainted my old friend Mr <Ralph> Sheldon of it (who loves you and told me that he sawe you) and I have desired him to acquaint his cosen the Archbishop of Canterbury about it. He will doe it, but he saies he knowes (for reasons of State etc.) he will not doe any thing in it. I also told Mr Dugdale and Mr Ashmole of it, who are both sorry for it and remember them to you ...

My *Templa Druidum* and *Chorographia Antiquaria* (or *Miscellanea Antiquaria*) is with Dr Locke [John Locke, the philospher] at my Lord Chancellor, who is much importunate with me to print it; and he will be at the charge him selfe, but I shall respite it till the later end of March, by which time I shall know what Mr Ogilby and I shall doe. I find Mr Ogilby very inconstant: but printed it shall be one way of the other by midsommer next. But it would be too much honour for such a poore scribler as I to be enrolled with those great Authors of Trinity College, but if you doe name me, I shall be much obliged to you. 'Tis pity such things should be lost ...

I am just now returning to my monastery at Hethfield.

Mr Hobbes has gott his printed works bound to send to Mr Pulleyn [Josiah Pullen, vice-principal of Magdalen Hall] together with a civill letter. It would not be unhandsome if he gave him thanks. The old gent is strangely vigorous for his understanding still: and every morning walkes abroad to meditate. He has writt a treatise concerning Lawe, which 8 or 9 yeares since I much importuned him to doe, and in order to doe it gave him the Lord Chancellor Bacons Maxims of the Lawe: now everyone will doe him the Right to acknowledge he is rare for definitions, and the lawyers building on old fashioned maximes (some right, some wrong) must needs fall into severall paralogisms. Upon this consideration I was earnest with him to consider these things; to which he was unwilling, telling me he doubted he should not have dayes enough left to doe it.

So I will conclude to you as I did to Mr Hobbes when I presented the foresayd booke of the Lord Bacon, when I puut him upon that Designe: *Fungar vice cotis acutum/Reddere qui ferrum valet exors ipse secandi* [I shall perform the function of a whetstone, which can make things sharp although it cannot cut itself. Horace, *Ars Poetica*, 304]. God blesse your undertakings.

Yrs yrs JA (F39, 195)

The *Templa Druidum* formed the first part of the work which Aubrey later called *Monumenta Britannica,* eventually comprising four parts. John Locke, who was at this time Secretary of Presentations to Shaftesbury, must have been very impressed by the *Templa Druidum* and *Chorographia* to offer to have them printed at his own expense and he persisted in his attempts to get them published right up to the time of Aubrey's death. With characteristic procrastination Aubrey missed the opportunity of having them published at this time, but in fact there was a great deal of work to be done on them before they were fit for the press, and he was expecting to be fully occupied by Ogilby for some time ahead.

Wood had promised to mention him amongst the authors of Trinity if *Templa Druidum* was published by the time his book came out; hence Aubrey's anxiety to convince Wood that it would be published by midsummer. But of course it was not, and Aubrey made a desperate plea again the following November:

> I thank you most lovingly for the honour you doe me in perpetuating my name: but I am sorry my *Templa Druidum* is not printed, which had [been] but for J.O[gilby]. Could you not name it to be *sub prelo* [in the press], or about to be so? It has layn at the Lord Chancellors this eighteen months. I thanke you also for your resentment [=sympathy] of my streights, and your kindeness shall never be forgotten. Good God, how much I am obliged to AW! (Tanner 456a, 14; 4 November, 1673)

But Wood was obdurate; and one can hardly blame him for this; *Monumenta Britannica* never was published.

Hobbes had been an undergraduate at Magdalen Hall (later Hertford College), but had never presented his works to the college, since Oxford as a whole and Dr Wallis in particular were bitterly hostile to him and all his works; John Wallis (1616–1703), Savilian professor of Geometry at Oxford and Keeper of the Archives, hated Hobbes and engaged in a pamphlet war with him on mathematical topics; Hobbes was no great mathematician and when he published a phamphlet in which he claimed to have squared the circle, Wallis tore it to shreds, but Hobbes remained unrelenting; in a letter to Aubrey of 5 March 1677, he writes: 'I was assured a good while since that Dr Wallis his learning is nowhere esteemed but in the Universities by such as have engaged themselves in the defence of his geometry and are now ashamed to recant it.' Nevertheless, Aubrey had negotiated with his friend Josiah Pullen, Vice-Principal, who said he would accept the gift on behalf of the college. Hobbes duly sent a bound copy of his works with a civil letter, a copy of which Aubrey included in his Life of Hobbes (B.L. i, 377). But the college proved sadly uncivil; eight months later Aubrey wrote to Wood:

'I am very much ashamed that no body sent Mr Hobbes thankes for his Booke (which cost him 25s), nay, not so much as sent him word that such a booke was received. I thought Mr Pulleyn would not have omitted it, though Dr Hyde [Bodley's Librarian] is Dr Hyde' (11 October 1673, F39, 231).

Hobbes did in fact at Aubrey's instigation write a work 'On the Laws' but refused to allow its publication, 'since it is imperfect at the end'; it was published after his death.

Aubrey knew his own shortcomings as a scholar but prided himself on being a 'whetstone' on which others sharpened their wits, and many of his distinguished friends such as Petty and Hooke recognised this quality in him.

Chapter VI

The Perambulation of Surrey 1673

At the beginning of April (1673) Aubrey wrote to Wood from Hothfield:

> I am glad your Booke goes on so well.
>
> I am shortly for London, but being incognito cannot be able to doe you that service I otherwise willingly would ... Long may my honoured friend Mr AW live, and that merrily, is the hearty desire of his most affectionate and faythfull friend and servant, Jo Aubrey.
>
> I have 3 other draughts of the severall views of Osney Abbey besides that I gave to the Monasticon in my Trunke at Kington by Easton but dare not trust my brother [William] with the key, for my bookes would be like butterflies and fly all about the countrey; but if you have occasion to make use of them, I will send for my trunke to Chalke. (F39, 199; 7 April 1673)

This letter gives the first hint of his dislike of his brother William, which was later to flare up into a terrible quarrel.

A week later he was still at Hethfield and clearly in a deep depression: 'I have a great mind to make my selfe once more happy in your so good and so ingeniose, innocent and friendly conversation: and whether ever I may a second time God knowes. The starres frowne untowardly on this Nation' (F39, 202).

He wrote from London in May, where he was continuing to try to answer Wood's queries. His depression had failed to lift: he attributes his state of mind to the influence of the planets in this his most uncompromising statement of his belief in astrology:

> London 14 May 1673
>
> Dear Friend,
>
> I came hither about a weeke since ... Mr Dugdale does but what is fitt in his Elogie [eulogy] of your worth, which will more and more encrease *occulto velut arbor aevo* ['like a tree with growth unseen', Horace Odes i.12, 45]: yet I am verily perswaded your disposition is naturally so sweet and even, that it will not inflate you ...
>
> I could wish my selfe with you this moneth for 2 or 3 dayes to relaxe and revive my dull dejected spirit, which now after this Quartile Aspect of Saturn and Mars will be better about Whitsuntide; for we are governed

by the Planets, as the wheeles and weightes move the Index of the Clock ... As soon as these ill Aspects are over and not before, I will treat with Mr Ogilby, who is a cunning Scot and must be held fast. (F39, 206; 14 May 1673)

In May Aubrey received his licence to survey Surrey as Ogilby's deputy. Armed with this imposing document, Aubrey prepared to set

Osney Abbey: engraving by Wenceslaus Hollar from a drawing commissioned by Aubrey: in Dugdale's Monasticon Anglicanum.
By kind permission of Bodleian Library

forth, but not without frequent postponements. May 24: 'About a fortnight hence I shall goe upon Surrey.' June 17:

> I shall not begin my journey till this day or to morrow sevenight, for the horse will not come up till next Saturday, and my brother (I thanke him) haz lamed my horse just as I have occasion for him; and a good handsome horse to doe me credit; so I shall be forc't to ride my brothers, a little nagge. I have gott a pretty youth to wayte on me that can write and read and loves ingeniose things and will be adroit for my service. I long as it were with a womans longing to see Oxford and you ... I am not yet free from the malicious aspects of Saturn, who will doe me no good yet 2 yeares: the delicate aire and diversion of Surrey will cure my lassitude of Spirit (I hope). (F39, 214).

June 24: 'I shall not goe into Surrey till to morrow sevenight, or the day before ... Dr Twisse desires to be kindly remembered to you and is sorry for your sake that you are so unworthily dealt with. Honest Anthony, never let your spirit be troubled; your worth and fame will surmount these envious mists that peevish leane pedantiq spirited men raise up ...'(F39, 217).

'Never let your spirit be troubled ...'; Wood was having a difficult time over the printing of his History; Dr Fell was making changes in his text and Richard Peers, an undergraduate of Christchurch, who was translating it into Latin, made things worse – 'a sullen, dogged. clownish and perverse fellow, and when he saw the author concerned at the altering of his copie, he would alter it the more and studie to put in things that might vex him and yet please his deane (Dr Fell)' (L & T ii, 200).)

July 5: 'On Munday (Deo volente) I intend to sett forth, the wet weather hitherto hindring me.' A final note, undated, appears to signal his actual departure: 'I have just now received a small viaticum of Mr Ogilby and am hasting for my journey.'

The *Perambulation of Surrey* enables us to trace his journey and follow his laborious efforts in transcribing inscriptions from tombs in churches and other monuments, but as far as letters go there is a month's silence, until he has arrived at the southern extremity of the county:

> Aug. 10,1673
> Stanesstreete-cause-way, neer Sussex
>
> Deare Anthony,
>
> I have had the Pleasantest Pilgrimage that ever any man has had I thinke since the Reformacion, and found many strangers very civill to me, much more then I did in Wilts; and am now accidentallly fell upon a countrey-man, the Curate of this place, who is exceedingly humane to me ...

In our Lady's Chapell at Trinity Church in Guilford is a sumptuous monument of marble of Archbishop George Abbott [Abbot's inscription quoted in full – whole page]. He was the son of a Sherman: his mother with child of him longed for a Jack (= a pike) and dream't that if she could eate a Jack, her son should be a great man: the next morning going down to the river (which runs by the howse, which is by the Bridge) with her payle to take up some water, a good Jack came into the payle, which shee eat up all of by her selfe. This is generally received for a truth. His Godfather sent him to the University

I shall goe next upon Sussex, if the weather holds goode; els, not, by reason of the untravellable wayes. After Sussex, advise whether I shall enter upon Berkes or Oxfordshire …

My respects to the Merry Gang. I intend before Christmas to perambulate Berks; therefore make what apparatus you can for me against that time. I sent you downe by the carryer halfe a score of Queries.

Tuissimus JA (F39, 221)

The 'delicate aire and diversion of Surrey' certainly had cured his depression and he was now in a state of euphoria, hyperactive and making wildly optimistic plans to survey another three counties before his contract with Ogilby ran out in October. In the past month he had covered a remarkable amount of ground and had assembled a mass of information. He was back in London a month later, in a rather more sober and realistic mood:

London, Sept 16,1673

Mr Wood,

I returned hither 2 or 3 dayes since and received yours of Aug.17 at Honest H. Coleys. I have a weekes worke or better left to do the other side of the Thames which I reserved to the last. I have taken a great deale of payns, but with much delight, and if Mr J.O[gilby] will be ruled by me to print the extracts of the Records in Tower and Domesday-booke, all which I gott for the asking, it will be a pretty piece …

I hope to come into Berks about 3 weekes hence. Mr Ashmole will assist me: after my returne out of Surrey, I shall know what I shall have. If Mr J.O. deales honourably with me, I will go forward into other Counties.

[Answers to queries, including several funerary inscriptions]

I have also as many to write but the post calls. I will send the rest.

Tuissimius JA (F39, 223)

Aubrey was by now becoming increasingly disillusioned with Ogilby: 'I feare Mr J.O. will show himselfe unworthy of me' (20 September 1673), and three days later:

London, Morrow after St Matthews Day, 1673

Deare Friend,

To morrow I am setting forth again to make an end and intend to returne in a fortnight. Never had man to doe with such a fickle and subtile man as J.O[gilby] ...You may easily imagine that I have religiously collected: and I have got the favour of a great Antquarian of Surrey to have all the extracts of the Tower for the whole countrey [i.e. county] which is not above a quire and half of paper finely writ. Mr Dugdale and Mr Ashmoll both say unless J.O. makes use of them, his booke will be a bable. This and many good things he will leave out too, because he will squeeze all England into 5 volumes. Perhaps some time or other my first copy with Records aforesayd and visitation of Surrey may come out by him or somebody els. 'Tis pity it should be lost. (F39, 229)

When Aubrey had studied the Records in the Tower and Domesday Book, he usually started each section on any town or village with a history of landholders etc. from the time of the Conquest and then proceeded to memorial records in churches, followed by notes on soil, springs, minerals, where appropriate, and remarks on natural history etc., besides describing any castles, noteworthy houses and archaeological remains. His was a massive but chaotic compilation of information. He revised it in 1691, but, as he says in the preface he wrote at this time: 'The papers are like Sybillina Folia. I shall not take the pains to digest them in better order (which would require the drudgery of another Transcribing) and now I set things down tumultuarily, as if tumbled out of a Sack, as they come to Hand, mixing Antiquities or Natural History.'

Aubrey left the manuscript with his other papers in the Ashmolean Museum. It was discovered by Rawlinson some twenty years after his death; he revised and expanded Aubrey's notes and published it in Aubrey's name in 1718. It became the standard reference book on Surrey for the next hundred years.

Aubrey soon heard that Ogilby intended to make no use at all of his material, as he told Wood in a rambling letter:

London Oct.11,1673

Dear Friend,

I beg your pardon that I have not at this time answered yours of Sept.23 and 28, but I began my little journey on Oct.3rd and after the third day either my horse brake out of pound at Esher or els was stolen. I have been in quest of him and cannot heare yet of him and yesterday came hither from Richmond on foote – and not so much weary (I thinke) as if I had road, and were it not for some critical coxcombes, I would as soone doe this worke pedestrian as equestrian. About the middle of next weeke I shall either buy or have a horse lent me by a friend.

Oct.16. I was interrupted from goeing farther in this letter of Oct.11. On Sunday last newes was sent me of my horse, which I went for to Kingston on Monday, and came back last night; his fees for pounds etc came to 8s. But I should have told you that on Sunday Mr O[gilby] told me he had altered his mind and would now make no use of me, but get what scraps he could out of bookes or by hearsay, and will not write above 4 or 5 leaves (at most) of any County. I asked him then for some consideration for my expence in towne all this time on his account and for sending downe my horse; for God, not a shilling. So I have perambulated Surrey to my very great content and am out of purse beside the 7li I had of him, 4 or 5li at lest. God deliver me from such men. Mr Hooke sayes he will next Spring bring him about again, but I do not much care, though I should have been glad to have surveyed Sussex ... My *Templa Druidum* will be printed in J.O.'s *Britannia*, but I am resolved to have my name to it, or would you advise me otherwise, to print it by it selfe, for what it may be worth, which is not much; is it worth 5s? I am heartily glad you did not deale with J.O., for assuredly he would have left you in the lurch ...

Adieu, Deare Friend; all happiness attend you,

Yours, JA

I am resolved to live all this winter as concealed as I can and try to step into some preferment or other, be it but indifferent, for I have Friends enough to direct me. God blesse us both.

Prithee let me know if the Dean of Wells is not inflated by his titles [Bathurst was now Vice-Chancellor]. I will not trouble you to be resolved of that query of his godly Lady. (F39, 231)

Ogilby's decision must have been a bitter blow to Aubrey, both because he lost an employment which carried with it a protection from arrest, and because he had so enjoyed the work, but his reaction was characteristically stoical. Hooke and Wren were indignant on his behalf, and Hooke hoped to bring Ogilby back to the original plan the next year. But although Ogilby had cooperated with Hooke, Wren and Aubrey in producing a list of queries which envisaged a major survey, he drew back when he found what such a work entailed. He had hoped to have his book in the press by November 1673 and this gave him time to do no more than produce better maps of Britain, and so he dropped Aubrey altogether. He and his agents had in fact surveyed in detail 25,000 miles of roads by the time his *Britannia* went to press in 1675.

Why Aubrey should ever have considered asking Ogilby to include his *Templa Druidum* in *Britannia*, it is hard to say; Wood advised him against doing this (A13, 261):

As for your Templa Druidum, I advise you to print it by it self rather then in another book; for if in another, the author of that book will carry away the credit. I wish I could see a copie of it before it goes to Presse, especially half a year hence when my work is finisht, and then I shall not onlie advise you what to do in yt, but in your Perambulation of Surrey ...

[More queries, on Merton men]

Vive diu sed vive deo [Live long and live for God].

AW (A13, 261 – no date)

In November Wood was working on a life of Hobbes for his history; Aubrey, living concealed in London, sent Wood Hobbes's two Latin *Lives*, one in verse, the other in prose; of the latter he says:

Of that in Prose there is no other copy in England, wherefore I desire your speciall care to keepe it safe, and the next Terme send it by your brother, or keepe it till I come to you: next Christmas would be a busy time, and your booke will not be over so soon. Were not May a better time, to walke to Botley and hear the winged choiristers sing? (Tanner 456a, 15; 8 November 1973)

The following week he wrote to Wood again, once more thanking him for promising to mention his *Templa Druidum* and thanking him for a 'token' (£5),

which came in a very acceptable time and I sacrificed half a pint of sack to you. For your token I returne you many thankes and would not have you putt yourselfe to any further charges. You have abundantly obliged me severall wayes already, and your antiqu. and exemplary Friendship is never to be forgotten by your assured and most affectionate Friend to serve you to my power, JA. (F39, 234; 15 November 1673)

Aubrey wrote to Wood the following month answering queries and asking him to present his compliments to Wren who was in Oxford, where he was Savilian professor of astronomy:

London, Dec. 9, 1673

Deare Friend,

I was yesterday to wayte on Sr Chr Wren but Sr Chr is at Oxon. Pray forgett not to present my most humble and gratefull Acknowledgement; for he is one of the necessariest Friends I have to preferre me and a complement from me by you at Oxon may be better remembered then at Whitehall, where he haz so much businesse.

Yrs JA (F39, 241)

Christopher Wren, though still Savilian professor, was at this time mainly engaged in the rebuilding of London after the great fire, as

Surveyor-General and principal architect for rebuilding the whole city; he had already produced plans for the rebuilding of St Paul's and had started on the rebuilding of the city churches (fifty-two in all). No wonder he had so much business at Whitehall; that he could still find time to help Aubrey is proof of the affection he felt for him.

One cannot fail again to admire Aubrey's generosity of spirit and disinterested affection for Wood; he was prepared to give all and despite his own desperate circumstances, which were to lead shortly to his arrest for debt, he expected nothing in return. When Ogilby had failed him and the future must have looked singularly black, he showed no self-pity but remained in good heart.

Chapter VII

Dr Fell's Foystings 1674

AUBREY WAS NOW WITHOUT PROTECTION from arrest and without employment, but his friends were more concerned about his perilous situation than he was himself. He was making little effort to conceal himself, judging from the entries in Hooke's diary, which show him attending meetings of the Royal Society and at coffee houses night after night. Nor had he yet made any attempt to 'step into some preferment'. His friends, desperate on his behalf, pressed him to take some action, as the following letter to Wood shows:

London, Febr. 23d, 1674

My good friend,

Oh Anthony, what worke doe the Executors and Widowes with Libraries which were so dearly beloved by their Masters! and oh that men would be more publiq spirited and make their hands their Executors and their Eyes their Overseers.

... Now let me take you to Scrutiny: Are you turned Rom. Cath. or no? You know that I am no Enemie to them, unless Irish Biggotts. That you are so was reported at the Vice-chancellors table (Mr Bathurst) and that by the Deane himselfe ... Well, I say that a little superstition is a good ingredient in governement. What publiq spirits are now left, nay, almost I ask, what common honesty? Among the Clergy, Humility and Charity are very rare; except you come to an honest bachelor parson.

Now I must unbosom my selfe and desire your friendly advice and counsel (which I have donne before now) what course of life to take. I have severall good Friends who are great men, that ask and chide me, saying, 'Have you found out any good place yet? but find it out, your Businesse shall be donne.' So I have lodged Queries in the Custome-house, Tower etc. But I am stormed anew, I am at my Witts end. They would now have me turne Parson and keepe an honest Curate, and I shall have a Parsonage of 200li. *per annum.* What doe you thinke of this? is it honourable, or prudent? Lord, how I should looke in a Cassoq! The Newes is that we shall have Warres with France; I doubt how strongly the Church of England stands; if it changes, what shall I doe? But this much they tell me and tell me truth, that I love not businesse, and riseing earling (early) is death to me. In this case [i.e. as a parson] I shall take no paines, enjoy my friends at London or Oxon, and have a gentile

Competency. Pray advise me by the next post what to doe, for I am so importuned that I could scarce sleep last night.

Pray burne or blot out some *arcana* [secrets] of AW and JA in this letter. (F39, 255)

Since he had become a friend of Sheldon, Wood was becoming increasingly subject to accusations of being a Catholic; he records in his diary: '6 Feb., Friday, at night, I was at the vice-chancellor's, Dr. Bathurst. He was very civil to me; but she said not one word, neither dranke to me, because shee thinks I am a papist, but shee is mistaken ... People avoid my company and shun me: every one tells me I receive not the sacrament' (L & T II, 281). Much as he hated Puritans ('sniveling saints'), Wood was never tempted to convert to Rome. Aubrey was far more inclined to do so, though from motives of self-interest rather than conviction. The proposal that he should turn parson did not appeal to him. He had a deep contempt for most of the clergy and he would not have found it easy to suscribe to the thirty-nine Articles; hence he asks, 'Is it honourable?' But it was a temptation; if he paid a curate to do the work, a common practice, he would still have had enough to live on and could have enjoyed his friends without pains. Wood must have replied promptly, advising him not to turn parson, for Aubrey wrote at the end of March:

London, March the last, 1674

Deare Friend!

I received your kind letter of advice of the beginning of March and am sorry I have been so long silent, first because when it came I was in some trouble under an Arrest, which (I thanke God) happened very well, but too long now to trouble you, for Providence provided better for me than I could have donne for my selfe or imagined; for I have a friend will undertake to manage my concern in Brecon and I shall pay my debts. Your letter is mislayd amongst a multitude of papers; not yet found. In short, I thanke you for your advice concerning the Cassoq, and it will be better for me to accept of 50li or 60li per annum, which will serve my turne.

Mr Robert Hooke (who writt the Microscopicall Observations) hath newly in print (in quarto, 4 sheetes) An Attempt to prove the Motion of the Earth. I hope it will hold.

[Miscellaneous information – mostly on Oxfordshire]

In May next I hope to take a Pilgrimage to Oxon to enjoy your leisure and good company for 2 or 3 dayes and heare the winged choristers sing ...

I am much troubled that I have been so long silent to you, partly for my trouble, and partly being engaged in writing the Catalogue of the

Repository of the Royal Society, which will hardly be finished by the beginning of May …

Vivas et valeas [Long life and good health],

Tuissimus JA (F39, 261)

On 5 March the inevitable had happened: '1674, die Jovis [Thursday], 5th Martii, 9h(ours) 15'(minutes) + P.M. J.A. arrested by Gardiner, serjeant, a lusty, faire-haired, solar fellow, prowd, insolent, *et omnia id genus* [and everything like that]' (Accidents). Hooke's diary entry is more succinct and more informative: 'March 5 Mr Aubery arrested for £200'; and four days later: 'March 9th Mr Aubery cleered etc.' We do not know who payed his debts or who undertook to manage his business in Brecon, possibly his cousin, Sir John Aubrey, of Llanthridyd. The arrangement may have settled his debts in Wales, but unfortunately he still had creditors in England.

Hooke's *Attempt to prove the Motion of the Earth*, in which he established the three basic laws of planetary motion, was to land him in bitter controversy with Newton (see pages 121–3).

Aubrey's friends of the Royal Society had found him another job – to catalogue their Repository, that is their Museum, a task he had still not completed fifteen months later.

Wood's book was due to come out at Oxford at the Act, the annual celebrations at which there were speeches, concerts and plays, in July. As the time drew near, Wood's indignation at Dr Fell's 'foystings' increased; Fell's alterations to Wood's account of Hobbes became the central issue:

> These additions and expunctions being made by the said deane of Christ Church, without the knowledge or advice of the author and quite contrary to his mind, he [Wood] told him [Fell] it was fitt Mr Hobbes should know, because that, his name being set to the booke and all people knowing it to be his, he should be liable to an answer. To this the deane replied, 'Yea, in God's name; and great reason it was that he [Hobbes] should know what he [Fell] had donne, and what he had donne he would answer for, etc.' (B.L.Hobbes i, 344)

Wood then wrote to Aubrey telling him how his account of Hobbes had been been mutilated; Aubrey passed this on to Hobbes. A violent controversy ensued, which Aubrey thoroughly enjoyed. He replied to Wood:

London, April 9th, 1674

Kind Friende,

I received yours concerning Mr T. Hobbes, which he has, and remembers him kindly to you and will be glad to see you when you come to Towne, but desires you will write to him a Letter of Complaint (as you did to me) concerning Dr Fell, and he will in an Answer vindicate himselfe, both which he will print with a booke, Homer Odyssey, which is shortly going to Presse. He makes verses every day and has his parts vivid still to admiration. I went to him on his birthday (which was then he said Good Friday) ... I shewed your letter to Sir Chr. Wren, Dr Twisse in multis aliis (amongst many others) and have heaped burning coals of Juniper upon his (i.e. Fell's) black scalpe; methinkes he lookes as if his face was boyled in his owne Galle.

Sr. Chr Wren did (quasi) intimate to me as if the Deane of Wells [Bathurst] was not resolute and couragious enough in his friendship of him [Hobbes]; what good can the Deane of Christchurch (Fell) doe him? or why should he stand in awe of that shotten-herring?

I long to be in Oxford for 2 dayes when your booke's donne, to enjoy your company. I am like to be spirited away to Jamaica by my Lord Vaughan, who is newly made Governor there and might desire to have me goe with him, and will look out for imployment worthy a Gent for me. Fough! The cassoq stinks; it would be ridiculuous. I can send into England every month or 6 weeks. (Ballard 14, 98)

Receiving no reply from Wood, Aubrey wrote again a fortnight later a letter which more or less repeats the previous one, including the plan to emigrate to Jamaica, to which he adds: 'The earl of Thanet would have me goe to his Estate in the Bermudas. I thanke God for his blessings' (Ballard 14, 99).

It is difficult to know how serious Aubrey was about his new thoughts of emigrating; Thanet was proposing to visit Bermuda for the sake of his health and wanted Aubrey to accompany him (F39, 259; Aubrey-Wood, 25 March 1674). In a letter of the following May, in which he discusses the plans for Hobbes's vindication, Aubrey adds: 'I doe think it will be my fate to go to America this summer' (F39, 268). But by the end of July he had decided not to 'roast him selfe for wealth'.

By April it had been decided that Hobbes's vindication was to take the form of an Epistle to Wood, which was to be bound into the book:

Most learned and dear Friend,

Our common friend J.A. has pointed out to me the additions and deletions that Dr John Fell of Christ Church has made in your book about the Antiquities of Oxford University, in the part which deals with my life. Where you describe my character as sober, he has deleted *sober* and substituted *harsh* ... Fourthly, where you wrote about my book Leviathan, in the first place, that it was famous in neighbouring countries, he has inserted 'for causing public harm'. Then, where you had written 'he wrote a book', he has inserted 'most monstrous'. This would have constituted

a very great injury, had he been either a qualified judge of learning or noted for any outstanding erudition at home or abroad …
I will not pursue the struggle in public writing. For I hold the testimony of my friends dearly, but take no account of the insults of my enemies. They can expunge my name entirely, if they like, from *The Antiquities of Oxford*; nevertheless I will receive the praise of the majority of present men of learning, and, I think, still more that of future generations. (Translated from Hobbes's Latin original; A9, 44)

In May Aubrey wrote to Wood on behalf of Hobbes to find out exactly how the Epistle would be incorporated:

London May 16, 1674

Mr Hobbes will print the Epistle at his owne charge: he askes where in your Booke it must come – in what page or etc. He stayed to know where it must come-in. When comes your booke out? To what Book-seller at Oxford shall he addresse the copies of his Epistle? If you make any reference to his letter, let Mr Hobbes knowe in what part of the Appendix, and to what sense.

I hope to see my mother and Brother at or about Whisuntide, and goeing or rather returning to see Oxon and my honored friend Mr Wood.

When Wood received a copy of the Epistle, 'he forthwith repaired, very honestly and without any guile, to the Deane of Christ Church to communicate it to him. The Deane read it over carelessly, and not without scorne, and when he had done, bid Mr Wood tell Mr Hobbes that he was an old man, had one foote in the grave, that he should mind his latter end, and not trouble the world any more with his papers' (B.L. Hobbes, i, 344–5).

When the copies arrived at Oxford, Wood's book was still not out; they were distributed amongst all the coffe houses and stationers' shops on 11 July, Act Saturday, when Oxford was crowded with visitors and en fête.

A copie forthwith came to the Deane's hands, who upon reading of it fretted and fumed, sent for the author of the History and chid him, telling him that he had corresponded with his enemie. The author replied that surely he had forgot what he had donne, for he [Wood] had communicated to him before what Mr Hobbes had sayd and written; whereupon the deane recollecting himselfe, told him that Hobbes should suddenly heare more of him. (B.L. Hobbes i, 345)

There was one blank page at the end of the History and this Fell filled with a virulent attack on Hobbes.

Wood was clearly nervous of Fell and worried about the outcome; he wanted to have back the letters of complaint he had written to Aubrey and which Aubrey had passed on to Hobbes, and he wanted to know whether the Epistle had been licensed for printing, and whether Will Crooke, the printer, would be discreet. Hobbes would not return the letters, but Aubrey could set his mind at rest on the other points:

London, July 23d,1674

My good friend,

The very next day after the receipt of your letter I repayred to Mr Hobbes, who remembers him to you, but will not diliver the letters. His Epistle the King himself licensed in the Pall-mall in St James's Park, where were about 30 of the Court attending him ... His Majesty was offended at the Deane's way ...

I have cautioned Will Crooke concerning you, and he sayth he knowes nothing but that Mr Hobbes sett him on the work, and Mr Hobbes will justify him.

The advice of your friends is to print a sheet or two of paper here, in vindication of your selfe in the matter of Mr Hobbes, to sett forth the Dean's dealing with you, and to be inserted in your Booke, which booke no body will buy without that and that many will buy that cannot or will not buy the booke. (Ballard 14, 103)

But Wood had had enough; bitter as he felt about it, he now wanted a rest: '25 July, Saturday, St James day, at 3 in the afternoon William Briscoe and I in Witham meed under a haycock. '*Deus nobis haec otia fecit*' ['A god has given us this peace' Virgil, Eclogue 1, 5]. 27 July, Monday, My book published at Oxon. Full of base things put in by Dr Fell to please his partial humour and undo the author' (L & T ii, 290). Ten days later (7 August) he departed to Weston to stay with Ralph Sheldon and remained there until 3 September.

Aubrey still pursued him with instructions about the Epistle in a letter in which he thanks him for sending a copy of his History:

London July 28, 1674

Worthy Friend,

I received yours of 26 Instant and on last Thursday sent a letter in answer to your two former, which I hope you received. Mr Hobbes went toward Derbyshire this morning, to whom I write the next post. Mr Crooke sent the Epistles (he tells me) to the Coffee howse at Oxon (one Balls), and in a letter about 3 posts since hinted to him that he need not be afrayd to disperse them (for fear of the Deane), for that the King licensed their printing.

I most heartily and sincerely offer up to you my thankfulness for your noble Present, and for the honour you have donne me therin; for like a wild Olive or polypedium, my name will live upon your never-dyeing structure.

Your friends and well-wishers here advise you (as I have hinted) to print a sheet or half sheet in your owne vindication, which everyone that buys your Booke will be sure to buy, and many will buy it that will never buy the Booke: PRAY OBSERVE IT. I will shortly send you my Bundle. Tell me when I shall come to you, or when you come to London.

Severall of my friends dehort me from Jamaica: for why should I at this time of day, and being of a Monastiq humour, make my selfe a slave and roast my selfe for wealth? Apage Satana [Get thee behind me, Satan!] Mr Hooke is designing to gett me the place of Chronologer of the City of London, which may be [MS torn] 80li per annum herafter, at present 40li and 'twill be agreeable to your faythfull servant JA (Ballard 14, 105)

Hobbes had been tutor to the Earl of Devonshire and lived in his household at Chatsworth or Hardwick where he died five years later at the age of ninety-one. Hooke had found Aubrey yet another job to persuade him to stay in England. For the time being Aubrey dropped all plans for emigrating; they crop up again several times later on as other friends offer him opportunities in the plantations, but from now on he does not seem to have been seriously tempted by these.

Chapter VIII

George Ent's Rhodomontades 1674–75

In the summer of 1674 George Ent, the friend with whom Aubrey had travelled in France ten years earlier, moved to Oxford and asked Aubrey for a letter of introduction to Wood, which he duly provided (Ballard 14, 107). Later in the month Aubrey sent Wood a letter containing a P.S. which was to cause considerable trouble:

London Aug.18, 1674

> Kind Friend!
>
> I have sent you by my worthy friend Mr Ent my manuscript *Historia Roffensia*, which I would have presented to the Bodleian Library together with *Mercurius Pragmaticus* when it comes to your hands, which will be about a fortnight hence. I have sent it with my draughtes of the Ruines of Osney Abbey … I beseech you keep them safe …When Osney is engraved I would have the original again.
> Tuissimus J.Aubrey.
>
> You would oblige Mr Ent to let him peruse Mr Hobbes Life in Prose [see B.L. i, 395–403]: he and his father have a very high esteeme for him. Pray let him have a copy of it: he haz given his faith to me no man shall have a copy of it after him. (Ballard 14, 108)

He had planned to give the *Historia Roffensia* to the library of the Royal Society, but they would accept only scientific books. *Mercurius Pragmaticus* was a weekly political journal running intermittently from September 1647 to April 1649; Aubrey had a complete set, now a rarity. These must have been amongst Aubrey's most valued possessions, which he now proposed to give to the Bodleian. With equal generosity he sent Wood his precious drawings of Osney Abbey; these he had commissioned when he was still an undergraduate at Trinity, shortly before the abbey was destroyed; it was his first attempt to save the past from 'the teeth of time' and they were very significant to him. Although the text of Wood's History was out, it did not include the illustrations; it was the regular practice to bring out the 'cuts' after the text, to be bound into the book later.

Aubrey soon regretted his rash offer to let Ent have a copy of the Life in Prose:

London Aug 26, 1674

Mr Wood,

I sent you two letters by my friend Mr George Ent, together with a bundle of bookes ... He was importunate with me to gett a copy of Mr Hobbes Life in Prose, which he would extort from me and I could not tell how to denye him; but I thinke it is not fitt. He is a very honest gentleman and his Rhodomontades you will easily pardon. (Ballard 14, 110)

Aubrey's last sentence suggests that he had some qualms about the meeting of his two friends, but at first things seem to have gone well enough. Wood wrote from Oxford soon after his return from Weston:

Sept 6, 74

Kind freind,

Upon my returne out of the Country after a month's absence, I found among others 4 of your letters, prospects of Osney, *Hist.Roff.* etc., all of which I shall safely keep and restore at your summons. Mr Ent left them at my lodgings in my absence: I have seen and shall be better acquainted with him at the place where he lodges, for there with some of my acquaintance doe I eat twice a week, and soe have don for the last year past ...

You would do well to tell me in your letters how my book is taken in London, what dislikes therein, what faults found etc., the which if you would do, I should take it very well and therein you would act like a friend. Pray if you find any faults in my book or can tell what writers are omitted, you would do well to enforme me ...

Yours, A.W.

Mr Sheldon lives like a prince, and I was entertained accordingly with all tenderness imaginable. (F45, 171)

Aubrey replied on 15 September:

Worthy and obliging friend!

I received your kind letter of the 6th instant. I hope the graver will doe Osney ruines handsomely. If you please, I will aske Mr Hollar whether his plate that he did for me in the *Monasticon* was burnt in the general Conflagration [i.e. the Great Fire of 1666].

Your booke is generally very well received, but would have been better, had not the Deane imbittered it soe much and soe often with his galle and spleen. But the Odium lyes on him, which, had not Mr Hobbes Epistle lett the world knowe the Deane's intermeddling, would have layn at your door. You have methinkes curtailed some eminent Lifes to much: e.g. James Harrington Esq., an eminent person and writer ... Mr Hooke told me (who has lookt over youre booke) that you have left out severall eminent men; you have not neither mentioned him, which I desired: England haz hardly produced a greater witt, viz. for Mechaniqs ...

Mr Ent is earnest to have a copy of Mr Hobbes Life in Prose, which upon 2nd thoughts I cannot think rational to assent to, and Mr Hobbes would be angry with me for it. But you may be pleased to let him read it. (Ballard 14, 111)

Wood must have answered that he had no information on Hooke; for once Aubrey is irritated by him and replies with rare asperity in his next letter:

London, Oct.24 1674

Mr Wood!

I beg your pardon for my long silence, having been avocated with some mundane affairs ... I am afrayd you loose my letters. I have in them given a full account of Mr Hooke, which if you have lost I will endeavour to retrieve. If I can, I will write today to Mr Ent. I desire he should peruse Mr Hobbes Life: but if he has a copy, it will fly about like lightning, and Mr Hobbes, who is something apt to be cholerique, upon just cause as to this, will be very angry, and I should lose his friendship.

I am right glad to heare of Dr. Plott's designe: it agrees so much with my Humour. I can much assist him in it, having a good *Penus naturalis* ['store of natural history'] of my owne collecting, which I dayly augment ... and I can furnish him with many fine things I have collected in Oxfordshire, which tell me wher I shall send them ...

The Cuckold of Aldington might have been pleased to have named me too, not that I value his Testimony, but he hath perused my MSS, and haz donne his businesse, and now a fart for me.

Vivas et valeas, tuissimus,
Jo Aubrey (F39, 282)

Dr Robert Plot, of Magdalen Hall, was writing a *Natural History of Oxfordshire*, which came out in 1677; he thereby anticipated both Wood's projected Oxfordshire and Aubrey's own *Natural History of Wiltshire*, which he had begun in 1656. But Aubrey with his usual generosity was delighted by Plot's design and offered to lend him all his own notes.

Thomas Gore (the Cuckold of Aldington) had brought out a catalogue of all authors who had written on heraldry, omitting Aubrey's name although he had used some of his work.

By November Aubrey had heard that Wood and Ent had met and seems to be encouraged by their first acquaintance:

London, Nov. 7, 1674

Mr Wood,

I received yours by Mr Wylds servant. I am glad you two good folke are acquainted, according to my desire. We talke of you every time we meet ...

Mr Ent is a good man and his Rhodomantades are innocent ... I intended to write to him to day, but Mr Wyld is now having me abroad with him to be merry.

Tuissimus J.Aubrey (Ballard 14, 114)

Six weeks passed before Aubrey wrote to Wood again:

London, Jan.12, 1675

My singular good Friend,

I have received two letters from you, viz. one of 8 Nov. and another of 13 Dec.; and I am very sorry and ashamed that I have not written sooner to you all this while: for no man living is more zealous for you than I am. But I have been so taken up about soliciting some Right I have in Wales, and looking after some preferment at Court that (and besides the dayes are so short and cold) I have scarcely had leisure ... Dr Charlton haz made a Collection of all the false Latins in your booke ... I would have you make such lines with red inke under mine or etc. letters, where are remarqueable things, and 'twill save a great deale of paines to read over again. (F39, 288)

We do not know what right Aubrey was soliciting in Wales; surely the entail case was not still lingering on? As for his attempt to gain some preferment at Court, we learn something of this in a letter from Thanet; this plan, to secure a sinecure through influence at court, like so many other of Aubrey's schemes, came to nothing.

He wrote to Wood in February, asking him to send some information about the Rollright Stones, a megalithic circle in the Cotswolds, for his *Templa Druidum.* Relations between Wood and Ent must have begun to deteriorate; no doubt Wood had been subject to Ent's rhodomontades when he refused to let him have the *Life in Prose.* Aubrey rather hopelessly attempts to patch things up:

When you goe or send to Weston next, you may informe me concerning Roll-rich stones, viz, the Diameter, how many yards or paces, and the height of the stones and the number, for my Templa Druidum.

I am sorry G. Ent and you have no better contexture of humours. I find him to be no great lover of Antiquities, but pardon him ... I would have you end all quarrels over a glasse of Sack. (F39, 265, 9 February 1675)

Wood, who had sent a 'token' to Aubrey by his brother, which Aubrey had not received, replied:

Feb.21, 75

Dear Sir,

I have received yours and am very much obliged to you in answering some of my Queries and that you are in readiness to give me satisfaction of the rest. Truly I account myself much in your debt and hope ere long to be quit with you. My brother I perceive is very slow in letting money goe out of his hand, or else minds more his owne gain than to do a small office for a friend. I shall take some other order if he doth not at this time leave some money behind him in London. You shall know more when he comes home. I thinke to goe some time this Lent to Weston and then, God willing, I shall view more severely the Roll rich Stones.

Dr Charleton they say hath made a collection of the false Latines in my booke and hath sent them to Oxon. The truth of this methinkes I would faine know and whether he hath taken notice of a false Latin by Dr Fell in the Epistle dedicated to the King.

Yours, AW (A13, 265r)

Four days later Aubrey was willing to capitulate to Ent's importunity and wrote telling Wood to let him see Hobbes's *Life in Prose*:

Feb.25, 1675

Deare Friend!

I sent a letter to you about a weeke since; I doe not at present remember the contents ... I thinke to satisfye Mr Ent's longing you must showe him the Life ... All men cry out against the Deane's spoyling your Booke ... In your next edition if you only mention my name in the Preface as you intended (and which the Dean I am confident scracht out) I shall be glad of the honour. I mean only shortly mentioned. (F39, 291)

Wood's patience with George Ent had now run out and he had no intention of showing *Life* to him; in a note scribbled on the back of Aubrey's letter he exploded:

You have alwaies told me since Mr Ent came from London, that you are sorry he and I have not a better contexture of humours – that you hope wee two have now a better correspondence, that you doubt not but wee now agree – etc., etc., such like. Now give me leave to tell you, that since he came from London last, a little before Xmas, he hath not taken notice of me nor spoke to me. The first time I saw him after his returne from London, I welcomed him, and when at dinner together I dranke to him, not taking notice <of> what before had passed: but he I say hath not returned to me the like civility, and therefore shews him self to be no good natured man. What? do you think that after he hath vented his simplicity towards me, I shall sneak to him – no, I will not. I have done enough already; besides had he any good nature, he would not be so quarrellsome in his liqueur, but being so, I have done with him, and am rather glad than sorrowfull for his displeasure ...

Your name I shall not mention in my Preface, but more at large in Trin. Coll., if so be you publish any thing before the next Edition. (A13, 265v)

Wood, no doubt, felt fairly confident that Aubrey would not have published anything before the next edition and that he would not have to acknowledge how much material Aubrey had provided.

Attacked from both sides, poor Aubrey was next subjected to a blast from Ent:

March 6th,1675, from Oxford

Worthy Mr Aubrey,

I could not get your *Pragmaticus* and your Italian book into the Publick Library without an additional number; and therefore I have given in your name 3 other books to Mr Hyde [Bodley's Librarian]; and he has accordingly entered all five in your name in the Publick Library book.

Sir, you see how I endeavour to gratifie you in all things wherin I am able to serve you, while in the mean time your animall here, A. Wood, does study to disoblige and affront me. Sir, I told you in my last that I would see him hang'd before I would ask him for Mr Hobbes Life and now I'll see him hang'd and damned before I'll do it. Why should he be courted to deliver the goods? You ought to command him to do it; God and Nature designed that fellow rather for a bricklayer than an Historian.

Sir, this is all for the present from

your affectionate friende and servant,
Geo.Ent. (A12, 105)

Aubrey wrote to Wood a letter in which he did his best to pour oil on troubled waters, although the second paragraph must surely have been intended to sting:

London, March 9, 1675

Deare Sir,

I received yours of 21 and 28 Feb. instant. I shall in a short time send you an account of your other Queries. For from being in my Debt, do not trouble yourself. I wish I were as able as willing to serve you. Now the dayes lengthen and the weather warmer I will fall to transcribe my MSS for the presse.

Mr Ent has Dr Charlton's collections of False Latins of the beginning of your booke, but there are I believe 10,000. He haz marked them all along, and I see not a page without false Latin or Solecisms, which are as bad.

I am exceedingly sorry for Mr Ent's strangeness to you; but 'tis confess't his friends must beare with him. (Ballard 14, 115)

The Latin translation of Wood's History, which Fell had insisted on despite the objections raised by Aubrey and others, was made by Richard Peers, a young student of Christ Church, who proved a lamentably poor Latinist. Relations between Wood and Peers had reached an all time low after Wood had returned from Weston in the previous October, even leading to fisticuffs (in which Wood came off best).

Ent seems to have been one of those unfortunate people who can do nothing right. Aubrey had sent the books via Ent to Wood, to be donated to the Bodleian; but Ent had kept them and now, being told he must donate a minimum of five books, he had made up the number by adding three others; the gift of one of these was to cause Aubrey acute anxiety three years later at the time of the Popish Plot (by which time Ent was dead); he wrote to Wood on 2 April 1679:

Tis a sad thing to doe with – but *de mortuis nil nisi* bonum [(say) nothing but good about the dead]; when I made my small Offertory to the Bodleian Library, Geo Ent, to fill-up the summe, putt-in *The Mystery of Jesuitism* or *Jesuits Moralls* (I knowe not which). Now I never meddled with Controversy in my Life, nor ever shall; I am only for Mathematics, Philosophy, and Antiquities. I wish it could be erased out and *Historia Roffensia* inserted in its stead. (F39, 318)

The book, which remained in the Bodleian, inscribed as a gift from Aubrey, could well have got him into serious trouble when anti-Catholic feeling was rife and the world was running mad. Besides being subjected to Ent's rhodomontades, Aubrey had also to apologise to Wood for Ent's failure to deliver the books to him:

May 18,1675

Mr Wood, London,

I received yours of May 5th ... Mr Marvell haz promised me to write minutes for you of Jo Milton ...

I intended and also sent the bookes by Mr Ent to be delivered **to you**, but it seemes he will have it his owne way. But though at present money is short with me, yet I would rather want more, then not freely make such a small Free-will offering upon such a Publiq account of doeing a mite of small good to the World.

I owe (duly) a kindnesse and respect to Mr Ent for his friendship and civility to me; but am so heartily sorry for his not being more a friend to him selfe and his owne reputation; and particularly in abating and lowering of his owne Judgement in his understanding of your praiseworthy paines and learning. But every Man to his Humour. I yet wish there could be a right understanding between you, and that you might make merry together at a Taverne. Hah! Mr Ent putts me in mind of the saying of Divine Plato, That perpetual drunkennesses is the reward of Vertue: and I do not beleeve that any Doctor at Oxon is halfe so happy in his Humour as he is ...

Deare Mr Wood, I am sorry to my heart that I cannot come to Oxon as I intended this Whitsuntide, wayting dayly upon Courtiers for preferment. I wish you a merry Whitsuntide and all happinesse, being sincerely

Your most affectionate and obliged friend,
Jo Aubrey (F39, 296)

'The saying of the divine Plato': Aubrey, tongue in cheek, refers to a passage in *Republic* Book 2 where Adeimantoes says that the Orphic teachers in their account 'lead the dead to Hades and sit them down and establish a banquet of the blessed and make them spend all time drinking, thinking that perpetual drunkenness is the fairest reward for virtue'.

Wood, by now, was certainly a difficult man whom it was dangerous to cross; perhaps the faults did not lie entirely on Ent's side. This is almost the last we hear of Ent who died a few years later; Aubrey, faithful to the last, was at his deathbed.

Chapter IX

The World Runs Madding 1675–79

FROM MAY 1675, there is a long hiatus in the correspondence between Wood and Aubrey; the latter left his 'cell', by which he means his 'monastery' at Hothfield, to stay with Sir James Long at Draycot Cerne, not far from Easton Piers, an old friend with whom he often stayed, a Fellow of the Royal Society, and a man after Aubrey's own heart: 'a gentleman absolute in all numbers ... Good swordman, horseman; admirable extempore orator pro harangue; great memorie; great historian and romancer; great falkoner and for horsemanship; on insects; exceeding curious and searching long since, in naturall things' (B.L. Long). Aubrey wrote from London on 19 June to tell Wood that he would be staying with Sir James Long until October and hoped on his return to see him in either Oxford or London (F39, 299). Meanwhile Wood was at Weston, where he was reorganising Sheldon's Library, from 30 July to 19 October.

In November, back in London Aubrey roused himself to write to Wood, from whom he had heard nothing for six months, offering once more to help with the *Lives* on which Wood was now engaged and asking him to pass on a message to Dr Plot; Plot (1640–1696) was writing a *Natural History of Oxfordshire* and planned to write natural histories of all the counties of England and Wales, plans which he abandoned when he was appointed the first Keeper of the Ashmolean Museum in 1683:

London, Nov.27, 1675

Dear Friend,

I writ to you from Sir James Long at Draycot in July last, but never heard from you since. I came last Wednesday hither from Chalke. I shall be glad to serve you in anything I can. I intended to wayte upon our Noble friend Mr Sheldon at Weston when you were there, but I had severall little pilgrimages which demanded my time whilest you were there and before the pleasant time of the yeare was spent.

I thought to have writ now to Dr Plot of Magdalen Hall, but being not certaine of his being there at present, I desire your kindnesse to enquire and to remember me kindly to him, and tell him I have writ out for him my Naturall History of Wiltshire, and of Surrey; and a sheet or two of other counties, and am sending to my cousen Hen. Vaughan (Silurist, Olor Iscanus) in Brecknockshire to send me the Naturall History of it, as also of other adjacent counties: no man fitter ...

Thus with my true love and respects remembered to you, I thanke you for all your favours; and shall be glad at your leisure to heare from you. Pray be brisque and lively, and let no melancholy creepe upon you. I find my goeing into the country hath donne me much good as to that ...

As you were sayeing, if I could be Principall of Gloucester Hall [now Worcester College], 'twere a fine way of ending my dayes in Peace and ingeniose Innocence. I would undertake to make it an igeniose nest, and would decoy thither severall ingeniose persons of either university, and some from beyond the sea. Well, as I sayd before, so I say again, be brisque.

Tuissimus, J. Aubrey (Tanner 456a, 19r)

Aubrey's disinterested generosity towards Plot is characteristic; he himself was working on a natural history of Wiltshire and had collected the relevant material for Surrey, yet he has gone to the trouble of making a copy of his notes and intends to put them all at Plot's disposal.

Henry Vaughan answered Aubrey's letter on 9 December: 'Tis a noble and excellent Disigne that your learned friend Dr Plot hath now in hand, and I returne you my humble and hearty thanks for communicating it with me. I shall take care to assist him with a short account of Nature's Dispensation here' (A12, 237).

Aubrey is clearly worried by Wood's long silence and concerned about his state of mind, and there is no doubt that the events of the previous year had made a deep mark on one who was always prone to melancholy and suspicion.

Wood must have told him in a lost letter about the lamentable state of Gloucester Hall and suggested that Aubrey should become Principal. In his Journal some years later Wood wrote: '1675 not one matriculated, 1676,7,8 not one scholar in Gloucester Hall; only the Principall and his family and two or three families that live there in some part keep it from ruin. The paths are grown over with grass, and this year (1678) the way into the Hall and Chapel nailed up with boards' (L & T ii, 398).

It is astonishing that this state of affairs should have been tolerated and persisted until the death of the incumbent Principal, Byrom Eaton, in 1693. Wood's idea that Aubrey should succeed him is not as fantastical as it might appear; he was well known and well liked at Oxford and had a reputation as a virtuoso although he had published nothing. Moreover, although in theory the Fellows elected their Principal, often an outsider was imposed on a college by the Visitor or by royal intervention; what was required to gain such a post was 'interest', and here Aubrey was well placed, being on close terms with Lord Pembroke, who had been Chancellor of the University, and a friend of other influential men.

Letters between Aubrey and Wood are less frequent now. Wood was often at Weston, or at Bath where he sought a cure for his increasing deafness. He does not seem to have been working on *Athenae Oxonienses* at this time. Aubrey did not write again until the following January:

London, Twelfeday 1676

My good Friend,

I sent a letter to you about the beginning of December [in fact, 27 November] but never heard from you: since, I heard from Dr Plot that you are not in Oxon. I guess therefore you are at Weston, and if so, pray present my most humble service and respect to my ever honoured friend Mr Sheldon. I wish you a merry and a happy New Yeare and shall be glad to serve you as ever. I have written the Naturall History (for Dr Plot) of Wilts and Surrey besides pieces of other Counties, ten sheets closely writt and shall send him more. As I was sending it to Oxon, our secretary [Oldenburg] hearing of it, thought fitt the Royal Society should first be made acquainted with it, which gave them 2 or 3 dayes Entertainment, which they were pleased to like. When you have nothing els to doe, favour with a line or two

Your old and faithful servant, Jo Aubrey (Ballard 14, 116)

The Classified Papers of the Royal Society include Oldenburg's transcriptions of the papers given by Aubrey under the headings: 'Observations made by Mr Aubrey of Surrey, Observations of Wiltshire by the same Mr Aubrey, read before the Society Dec.30,'75, and papers of Springs, Rocks, on Herefordshire, Somerset, and Gloucs' (Classified Papers vii, (i) 28; see T.P.W. 318–35).

Plot wrote thanking Aubrey, rather grudgingly since Aubrey's work overlapped with his own, in February (A13, 137). It is hard to judge how much of Aubrey's material Plot used; in any case he made scant acknowledgement, and Aubrey was later bitter about it, writing to Wood, he says, 'You know how Dr Plot served me.' Aubrey was unfailingly willing to help other scholars and lent his papers without a second thought, until he repeatedly found his generosity abused.

From January 1676 to the end of 1678 few letters passed between Aubrey and Wood. Wood spent more and more time enjoying the fleshpots of Weston. His visits to Weston became so prolonged that Sheldon was reduced to subterfuge to get rid of him; in his journal for 1679 Wood says: 'July 4, I went to Weston, tarried there till the 6 of November, at what time Mr Sheldon sent me home – pretended then to goe to London but returned in three days after' (L & T II, 455).

Wood was huffed by Sheldon's behaviour and did not seem to realise that he had outstayed his welcome.

Aubrey was busy enough in London, deeply involved in the affairs of the Royal Society and looking, rather half-heartedly, for some preferment.

In August 1676, after a gap of seven months, Aubrey wrote a short letter to Wood which led to a resumption of their correspondence:

London, Aug.22 1676

My deare and honoured Friend!

Though for a good while I have not written to you, doe not thinke that you are out of my thoughts, or that I am wanting in my Respects to you, which I shall ever continue as long as I live …

Had I wings (as it is in the *Vertuosos* (a play satirising the Royal Society)), I would fly to you: but my good wishes are continually sent. (Ballard 14, 118)

Wood replied immediately and Aubrey answered, again consulting him on the question of whether he should turn 'ecclesiastique':

London, Aug.29, 1676

Deare Friend,

I received your kind letter of 26th instant, and returne you my thankes for your enquiry after me.

Mr Sheldon haz been so civill to me as more than once to invite me to Weston, whither I should sooner goe than to any house in England. If I possibly can, I will come down to Oxon, but then how shall I get to Weston?

I am stormed at by my chiefest Friends afresh, viz Baron Bertie [later Earl of Abingdon, Aubrey's patron], Sir W. Petty, Sir J. Hoskyns, Bishop of Sarum etc to turne Ecclesiastique: but the King of France growes stronger and stronger, and what if the Roman Religion should come in again? Why then (say they) cannot you turne too? You (I say) knowe well that I am no Puritan, nor an enimy to the old Gentleman on the other side of the Alpes. Truly, if I had a good Parsonage of 200 or 300li per annum as they told me, it would be a shrewd temptation. *Sed praescribe, Tribati; quid faciam?* [But tell me, Tribatius, what am I to do? cf Horace Satires II, 1, 45]. Pray consider once more. The next weeke I shall goe into Essex with my good friend Mr Wyld but shall quickly in a weeke returne again and perhaps may goe with him to Worcestershire. (Ballard 14, 119)

We may assume that Wood again advised Aubrey not to turn ecclesiastic, for this scheme is never mentioned again. Aubrey wrote again on 11 September, sending his respects to Mr Sheldon (with whom

Wood was staying), 'on whom (if I possibly can) I will wayte, if I knew you would be there' (F39, 301). In the event Aubrey postponed his visit until autumn 1678, with unfortunate consequences.

On the back of this letter is scribbled a P.S. which shows how the anti-Catholic feeling was mounting in the country:

> If you die, or, one knowes not some time or other, the World runs madding, your papers may be sifted and examined. Therefore *ex abundante cautela* [as an extreme precaution], I would entreat you to burne (or blott out) a passage in a letter of mine about 1674 or 5 wherein I expresse my friendship to the church of Rome – God blesse us from another rebellion – 'twas when I was invited to take a benefice. (F39, 301)

The letter he refers to may be that of 23 February 1674 (see page 55), but several other letters would have been incriminating in the event of a witch-hunt such as that which was actually to occur during the Popish Plot. As Wood was widely believed to be a Catholic, Aubrey's fears are quite rational, and Wood's papers were in fact searched during the panic caused by the Plot. Despite Aubrey's entreaties, Wood never did blot out incriminating passages but preserved all his letters uncensored.

From 1677 only three letters survive from Aubrey to Wood, none of much interest. Six months passed before he wrote again:

> London, June 6, 1678
>
> My Worthy Friend,
>
> I have you often in my thoughts, but have not written to you for want of matter, and was unwilling to give you needless trouble. I am satisfied that you doe believe I love you and have a great esteeme for you and should be glad to serve you. I have a good mind one time or other to enjoy a weeke or two at our honoured friend's at Weston ...
>
> I desire you to keepe safe the Prospect of Osney Abbey ...
>
> My old friend Mr Francis Potter author of the Interpretation of 666 dyed between Easter and Whitsontide last. His bookes were sold under 3li.
>
> Tuissimus, J.Aubrey

Receiving no reply, he wrote again the following month after meeting Sheldon in London:

> London, July 9, 1678
>
> My deare Friend,
>
> I sent a letter to you about 6 weekes since to which I have yet received no answer. I sent the letter to Oxon, but I understand by my noble friend Mr Sheldon that you were either at his house or at Bathe, where the

waters, I hope, have donne you some good … Pray let me heare from you as soon as you can. Direct your letter to Mr Hooke's lodgings at Gresham College.

Wood, after returning to Oxford, replied:

Thursday July xi

Dear Freind,

After my returne from Bathe, where I have been a great while but find no fruits, I found yours at my Lodgings of 6 of June, to which I answer: 1. That there is no man will be more welcome at Weston than you. 2. As for the prospects of Osney Abbey, I shall preserve them safe … I thanke you also for Harrington's Epitaph; and if you can help me to any other Oxford men's epitaphs, you will doe me a singular favour.

In my returne from Bathe I called upon Malmsbury, where I beheld those majestic ruins …

I remaine your loveing friend, A.Wood

Since my writing of this letter, I received another from you dated 9 July. I come to Weston about the middle of August …

On 17 August Aubrey at last wrote to Wood with firm plans to visit Weston in September:

London Aug.17, 1678

Mr Wood,

I received your kind letter of July xi for which I thanke you. I am sorry to understand by you that you have not found more good by Bathe. Remember that I tell you a Recipe that hath donne great cures for deafnesse on severall, and I hope may have this effect on you; 'tis cheap, easily prepared, and without danger.

Pray give my very heartie and affectionate thankes and respects to our ever-honoured friend Mr Sheldon. I intend (Deo volente [God willing]) to leave London the first weeke of September and stay 2 or 3 dayes at Oxon and shall then make bold to send to Weston and accept Mr Sheldon's favour of a horse. (F39, 311)

For once he more or less observed his schedule, and he could scarcely have chosen a more unfortunate time to be staying at the house of a prominent Catholic.

Titus Oates made his depositions that the Jesuits were plotting to set fire to the City, murder the King, and conquer England by Irish and French arms, on 28 September; the whole country was immediately in uproar; the world, as Aubrey had feared might happen, 'ran madding'. While Wood and Aubrey were staying quietly at Weston, on 12 October 'Sheldon's house searched for armes, and were carried away by 6 men under the command of Sir Th. Mordant, on a plot of the Papists discovered a week before at London' (L & T ii, 423). Aubrey, always inclined to be nervous, left Weston promptly, touching Wood for a loan to get him back to London: 'October 15th: Lent Mr Aubrey at his going from Weston 3s6d – he saith hee'l pay my brother in London' (ibid). Wood stayed on at Weston until 28 November; whatever his faults, he did not lack courage. A week before he left, on 22 November, Aubrey's old friend Thomas Mariet, now High Sheriff of Warwickshire, arrived at Weston with a warrant from the Privy Council and arrested Sheldon and took him to Warwick gaol.

On his return to Oxford Wood was immediately summoned by Dr Wallis, who 'took away all writings and registers that I have had in my keeping 18 yeares for feare that they should be seised on, he supposing that I might be in the plot because Mr Sheldon was lately clapt up in prison. – A man that is studious and reserved is popishly affected' (L & T ii, 424). Three days later the Vice-Chancellor came to his lodgings with a beadle and two men and searched his study; nothing incriminating was found, but the next day he had to take the oath of supremacy and allegiance at the Vice-Chancellor's office.

Oxford was in a fever of excitement, as Pigot, a young Fellow of Wadham who admired Aubrey, had told Aubrey in a letter of 3 November: 'Every corner is now filled with rumours concerning the Plot, in so much that all other discourses seem to be silenced, but I hope learning will still go on and flourish and universal character not be neglected while advanced by yourself and learned friends' (A13, 118; 3 November 1678); he wrote again the following January: 'These troublesome and disordered times take away all thoughts of learning whilest our minds are amused with plots, policyes, and rumours' (A13, 119, 5 January 1679).

Sheldon was treated well enough in gaol, as Aubrey told Wood: 'I am sorry for Mr Sheldon but beleeve and hope him innocent ... I had a letter from Mr M(ariet), the high Sheriff, to that purpose, who was very civill to him' (F39, 312; 5 December 1678). By the following April he was free again; in June he met Aubrey in London: 'Yesterday came to me honest John Aubrey, whose head is so full it will not give his tongue leave to utter one word after another. I assure you, he is to my appearance as mad as anyone almost in the university of Bedlam' (F44, 111; Sheldon-Wood, 27 June 1679). Sheldon refers to Aubrey's stammer, which must have been made worse on this occasion by embarrassment, for he had committed some unpardonable indiscretion in a letter to Mariet, for which he was taken to task by Wood; we do not know what this indiscretion was but it concerned Sheldon; these were dangerous days, when, with Oates on the rampage, a loose word or two could bring a man to the gallows. Aubrey wrote to Wood remorsefully, trying to excuse his conduct:

London June 26, 1679

My good Friend,

I received yours of Corpus Christi day, for which I most kindly thanke you, though the later end of it troubles me most of any letter I ever received in my life time. When I writt that letter to Mr Mariet, I writt it on a Thursday night late, at our Club. Mr Hooke delivered me a chiding letter from Mr M[ariet], that I was slow of my pen and desired me to write him some newes. Of our Royal Societie Club, we have severall Parliament men and Courtiers, persons of great intelligence [i.e. very well informed], who commonly broach the newes first to us: and then in order to Mr M's desire, and my head being fuller of good wine than Prudence, immediately at the Stationers shop by the Taverne, I gave their account, which, though I believe it to be true, yet as soon as I had sent the letter to the post-house, I was troubled with an impulse of Spirit that I had not donne well: though it was to my old acquaintance and intimate friend from boyhood …

As concerning the Queen, there is shrewd evidence against her; severall of our Members have copies of the Deposition, which will certainly cut her off, if she stayes: but, they sayd that she will goe to the waters of Burbon [=Bourbon-les-Bains], and so into her owne Countrey (Portugal). The judges were sent to consult yesterday; some sayd they adjudged it not fitt for her to goe.

This day I sawe my honoured friend Mr Sheldon, who told me he would write to you and that he goes out of towne shortly. I would more easily incurre any ones displeasure then his, he is so worthy and honest a gent …This letter I now write by way of easing my troubled mind, as by confession. (F39, 328)

It is not difficult to envisage a rather drunken Aubrey penning the offending letter at the Stationer's shop, thoughtlessly hoping to please his old friend Mariet by passing on rumours put about by some of his grand friends. But it was not the time to dabble in indiscretions; the wildest rumours were accepted as true. The Queen was accused of plotting to poison the King and convert the country to Catholicism; but Charles put no faith in Oates's calumnies and saved her by dissolving Parliament. Aubrey seems ready enough to believe the story and had already passed on to Wood an extraordinary piece of scaremongering:

London, June 5, 1679

Mr Wood,

Yesterday on the Old Exchange 'twas reported that in the Catholic Countreys there is a Sodalitie of Devotos that goe up and downe begging

> for money to carry on the Warre in England for establishing their Religion, and that they have gotten about two million. They weare crosses, and a Crowne of Thornes on their head. (F39, 324)

This passage comes from a longish letter containing answers to many of Wood's queries and ends with apologies for not having done more: 'The truth is that I and Mr E.Wyld doe growe a little lethargiq, but however beleeve that no man has a greater esteeme for you then Your old doting friend to serve you, J.A.'

Aubrey was now undergoing a long period of what he calls lethargy: 'I do often chide my selfe as I lye abed to consider how much time Mr E. Wyld and J.A. doe loose, and growe lethargiq' (F39, 316, 9 April 1679). Things were little better the following December when he next wrote to Wood: 'I had long since given you an account of all (or most) queries, had I not been a good while in the Countrey. The Sun being now entered into Capricorn will begin to mount a little higher and consequently I shall be less lethargiq and vigorous in answering your queries' (F39, 331, 17 December 1679). But the letter contained news which was soon to stir him from his lethargy into a spurt of furious activity: 'Mr Thomas Hobbes dyed at Hardwyck (speechless 6 dayes) Dec. 4, buryed 6. I have sent for a more full acount as to Funerall, Will etc ... I must desire you with all possible care and speed to send me his Life in Prose, which I am to continue with halfe a score lines.'

Chapter X

The Life of Hobbes 1680

AS SOON AS WOOD HEARD OF HOBBES'S death, he had written reminding Aubrey that some fourteen years earlier Hobbes had, at Aubrey's instigation, written his Latin *Life in Prose* and had told him to 'put it out' in his (Aubrey's) name after his death; this *Life* went up only to 1651 and would need updating. Wood saw here an opportunity to take his revenge on Dr Fell. Aubrey's reply to Wood's letter suggests that it had touched some spring which released him from his lethargy and rendered him positively euphoric, as he rehearsed the attack he would make on Fell, sometimes breaking into Latin, which would be the language of the additions to the *Life*:

London, St John Evan. die(27 Dec.),1679

Deare Friend,

You very much obliged me in your last, for your excellent advice, and putting me in the right way: and to doe your selfe and others Right. Wherefore please send me up all the Matterialls you can; for as you very well and truly say, his Life in Prose reaches but to 30 yeares since, and the transactions between Dr J. Fell and us is by no means to be omitted. Scurrilous Epistle of Dr Fell: I will gett Dr W.Pope to give one lash for his brother the Bishop of Chester [John Wilkins]: he haz a divelish sharp pen. I am as good as promised the assistance of Sir Geo Ent, for his Latin stile. He was a zealous admirer of both Mr Hobbes and Bishop Wilkins. I will gett it licensed by the Royal Society, for the Bishop's chaplaine will never doe it, or if the R.S. cannot doe it, print it in Holland or Scotland ... Must I sett my name at length, or J.A.? Ought not I to make mention that 'twas at my request (about 15 yeares since) that he writt his life and that he intrusted it with me, as his countrey-man, and ancientest acquaintance of his Countrey (from 8 years old)? Should not his Epistle to you be inserted? ... I will be zealously industrious in it and thanke you for your assistance. I hope we shall be sufficiently revenged of the Doctor [i.e. Fell]. *Rumpatur quisquis rumpitur Invidia* ['May every man who bursts with malice be burst himself']. Could a man have imagined such a Ghostlike ghostly father, so continuall and assiduous in the prayers of the Church of England, that made Almighty and most mercifull Father nauseous to his Lodgers (viz. 6 times a day), that upheld the Arke in the late times, that *tantam pomposam sanctitatis speciem gereret* [put on such a pompous show of sanctity], I say, could one have thought that this great Exemplar of Piety, a walking Common prayer-booke, could have made such a breach in the Moralls and Justice? and to have such a pruritus [itch], (or what worse shall I call it?) in the Tyranny of the Presse, and in scratching-out authors' due prayses, and expunging and interponing? that have made the Universitys worse thought of then ever they were before? Who can pardon such a dry bone? a stalking, consecrated engine

Portrait of Thomas Hobbes by Michael Wright, by courtesy of the National Portrait Galley, London

> of Hypocrisy etc. – tell me if I rayle well. How much should go in? this is but a rude, bold touch, to use the Paynters terme of art. (F39, 327)

Walter Pope, step-brother of Wilkins, was a fellow of Wadham and Professor of Astronomy at Gresham College.

On the back of this letter he answered some queries of Wood's and adds: 'I would have you acquainted with Mr Halley of Queen's College, whose worth I recommended to our Freind Mr Pigott.'

Edmond Halley (1656–1742) had at the age of twenty sailed to St Helena and laid the foundations of southern astronomy; elected FRS in 1678 he became a friend of Aubrey, who wrote to him in 1679 recommending him to study astrology, to which he replied with courteous irony:

> Sir,
>
> Mr Pigott dilivered yours to me ... As to the advice you give me to study Astrology, I profess it seems a very ill time for it, when the Arch Conjuror Gadbury is in some prospect of being hanged for it [Gadbury, one of the leading astrologers of the time, had just been arrested for complicity in the Meal Tub plot]. However I went to the Library and looked out the booke you recommended to me which I find to be published in 1557, so that I doubt not that the more modern Astrologers having more experience of things have added to him considerably. However, on your recommendation I will read it on.

He later became a close friend of Newton and published *Principia* at his own expense. In 1721 he was appointed Astromomer Royal.

Three days later Aubrey had some misgivings about this exuberant outpouring and wrote again to Wood rather more soberly, though even in this letter he was nearly carried away on a flood of invective:

> London, Dec.30,1679
>
> My honourd Friend,
>
> I writt a hastie drolling letter to you by the late post, which I hope you have considered. I am infinitely pleased at the Opportunity of doeing you Right, and revenging my selfe on that early-rising Common-prayer man (who vies with the bell-ringer) and vigilant Inquisitor J.F[ell]. I would desire you to draw-up the Life and Reflections as you shall best thinke fitt: no man els can doe it so well, and let the World know how egregiously you have been abused ... I would (I say) earnestly entreat you to drawe up a skeleton ... Sir George Ent hath promised to assist me in it, which will be easier to him when you have provided the ὑλή [material], for he will have only the trouble to word it ...You will be pleased to collect all the minutes that you received from Mr Hobbes when you writt your Booke.

> In 1665 or 1666 I told Mr Hobbes that I would make bold to desire him to write his owne Life: for it would be written by others and not well, and perhaps spightfully ... He thanked me for my advise and told me he would doe it, and that he would intrust it with me (his Countrey man) to publish it ... I shall rest in Peace when I have donne this good Deed. (F39, 334)

Soon Wood received yet another letter, countermanding previous arrangements, since Crooke, Hobbes's publisher, had received from James Wheldon, his executor, an updating of the *Life* by Hobbes himself (F39, 335; 1 January 1680). But this version would not do as it stood; Aubrey explains to Wood later in the month:

> London, Jan.17, 1680
>
> Deare Friend!
>
> I received your kind letters and all the papers, which I keepe on my table, and shall, when I have donne with them, restore them to you with thankes. Mr Hobbes's Executor sent his Life to Mr Crooke, somewhat altered from that which I had, but it reaches not much lower ...The Life being written in the third person, and much in Mr Hobbes's prayse, they conclude must for prudence and decency sake come abroad by another person; and they have pitch'd upon me, being his countreyman and old acquaintance. I have communicated these intrigues to no body but Mr Hooke (who will be secret) and Mr Crooke. Both of them agree to have the Life suddenly printed with a little short Preface, to which whether J.A. or els anonymously, we will be advised by you. To be sure, 'twill sell well; then, Mr Hooke advises me, in Easter terme when the 500 copies are pretty well spent, to reprint it with my Commentary (Mr Hooke likes it). (F39, 337)

Aubrey's role is now clear; he is to write a Commentary on Hobbes's own Latin *Life in Prose*, developing it and bringing it up to date. But Hooke very wisely, in view of Aubrey's inability to keep any deadline, wants the first edition to be printed at once without Aubrey's Commentary. The Latin *Life* would certainly have given Hobbes's enemies material for mockery, if it had come out in his own name; it is a positive panegyric of his own character and works, though it stops short of praising his physical appearance. On the back of this letter Aubrey adds a long P.S., in which we have the first mention of Dr Richard Blackburne, who was eventually chosen by Aubrey to write the Latin Life of Hobbes; we also learn that Aubrey had collected materials for a life of the Elizabethan astrologer John Dee five years before and of the mathematician William Oughtred:

> These are to advise you that I am lately enformed by a very learned

> young friend of mine (Dr Blackburne) that a learned and able person in this City (whose name I know not yet) is setting forth the Lives of severall Illustrious modern writers, e.g. Sr H. Spelman, John Dee, Mr T. Hobbes etc Roger Bacon. Some yeares since I did with much diligence and care make considerable collections for the life of my cosen John Dee ... I also collected diligently of the famous mathematician Mr W. Oughtred's sonnes and daughters and neighbours ...
>
> I growe more and more active as the sun growes higher, and do something remit of my Dormouse conversation. 'Tis the last worke I can doe for so worthy and honoured a freind, and by your helpe and favour my name (by it) may live.
>
> Dr Oates is implacably angry with the Bishop of Oxon [Dr Fell] for his slighting of him at Oxon and speakes reproachfully of him and sayes of him what I will not more enlarge in writing. Pray speake to Mr Pigott to bring you acquainted with that prodigious young Astronomer Mr Edm. Halley of Queens Colege, who beside his great learning is a very good natured man, and take Memoires of his Life from himselfe. (F39, 337v; 17 January 1686)

Oates was still on the rampage, though his influence was waning; Aubrey seems to be rather shocked by his attack on Dr Fell but can hardly have been displeased to see the latter mauled.

A month passed, during which Aubrey sent the manuscript of his Commentary to Sir George Ent who returned it without comment after keeping it for a week (Ent was now eighty-six and could scarcely be expected to write the Latin version of the proposed *Life*, much as he admired Hobbes). Aubrey then tried to persuade his old friend Dr Charleton to undertake this task without success.

> So about four dayes since I pich't upon an admirable young man ... Dr Blackbourne M.D., one of the best scholars in London of his age, and philo-Hobbes ...I have writt 3 copies (improved) of Hobbes's Life. I did not thinke I could have been so copious; it will be at least 8 sheets, and nothing there that is in the Latin one [i.e. Hobbes's Latin autobiography]. I shall not be able to finish the faire transcript till Thursday and will certainly (Thursday night) deliver it at the Oxon-armes to be sent to you. I desire you to give your opinion on the blanke pages and to doe it and returne as soon as conveniently and possibly you can. As I enlarge on Mr Hobbes life writt by him selfe, so Dr Blackburne will make use of all my Supellex [= material] doeing me the right to quote me and will doe you all imagineable right. (Ballard 14, 125; 10 February 1680)

Aubrey envisaged a happy cooperation with Blackburne, whose function was to produce a Latin version of Aubrey's Commentary, for which Aubrey himself would receive due credit; but sadly Blackburne became 'ungovernable' and Aubrey allowed the grass to be cut beneath his feet.

An undated letter from Aubrey to Blackburne has survived together with the manuscript of Hobbes's *Life*, which must have been written shortly after Aubrey had asked him to cooperate; Aubrey, intending to send him a draught of his Commentary, asks him to act as his 'Aristarchus'; he is still very undecided what form his *Life* shall take:

> Dr Blackbourne!
>
> Pray advise me whether 'twould not shew handsomest to begin with a description of Malmesbury, and then to place Mr H(obbes's) Pedigree?
>
> But, with all, should not "Thomas Hobbes was borne at Malmesbury, April ... 1588" be the initial and textual line?
>
> Shall I in the first place putt Mr H. life donne by himself? (If so, whether in Latin or English, or both?) Or else, shall I intersperse it with these animadversions?
>
> I could begin with a pleasant description of Malmesbury, etc. (all new and untoucht) 14 leaves in octavo, which his verses will lead me to, and which Ant. Wood seemes to desire.
>
> Pray be my Aristarchus, and correct and marke what you thinke fitt. First draughts ought to be rude as those of paynters, for he that in his first essay will be curious in refining will certainly be unhappy in inventing.
>
> Doctor, I am your affectionate and humble servant,
> J.A.

To this he added a scrawled query:

> Should mine be in Latin or English or both? (And by whome the Latin, if so?) Is my English style well enough?

It seems that Aubrey never despatched this letter, which came into Wood's hands together with the manuscript of the *Life*. Opposite Aubrey's last query 'Is my English style well enough?' Anthony Wood has jotted, 'It is well.' If Wood could not aspire to literary grace himself, at least he recognised it in Aubrey's work. Meanwhile William Crooke, learning rather late in the day that another (Dr Bates) was planning to write a life of Hobbes, wrote a frantic note to Aubrey, warning him to hurry, if they were not to be beaten to the post:

> Feb. 16, 1680
>
> Sir,
>
> This day I was at Jonathans Coffee House from 12 of clock until nigh one to meet you or Dr Blackborne to acquaint you that Mr Hobbs his Life is adoing by anothers hand. Therefore we must make all hast possible or else we shall be powerless. (A12, 86)

The next day Aubrey sent Wood yet another draft, but the letter accompanying this shows that far from making 'all hast possible', he has so enjoyed writing his commentary on Hobbes that it has inspired him to embark on yet another project, the lives of his closest friends amongst the Virtuosi:

> London Feb.17,1680
>
> Mr Wood!
>
> I hope I have transcribed this pretty true. I thought good to send it to you ... Mr Blackbourne (though unknowne to you) is much your friend and will doe you all imaginable Right. In all England we could not have alighted on such another. But he will not write one line till he heares from you ... I hope you like my commentary pretty well; I did not thinke I could have been so copious. I have yet more things to add, out of letters and Memorandum bookes ...
>
> On Sunday night it came into my mind to scribble a piece of paper close, which I shall enlarge (much), viz. the Lives of the worthy and ingeniose Sir W. Petty from his cradle; Sir Chr Wren the like, as also Mr Robert Hooke.
>
> The Lives of Sr H. Spelman, J. Selden (amongst others with Mr Hobbes) will be putt forth by Dr Bates. Contribute your knowledge. Dr Gale will give you an account of Roger Bacon. Will my libri A and B [i.e.the two books of the Wiltshire Antiquities] doe you any service? God prosper all your Endeavours and Illucrubations. Pray remember me to Mr Ralph Sheldon; and let me know when you are there. (Ballard 14, 126)

Aubrey is clearly on a high and was to remain so for several months. He sees good in everything – in Blackburne, in Bates (far from viewing him as a dangerous rival, he tells Wood to assist him), in Wood's return to the *Athenae Oxonienses*; in this mood Aubrey saw no limits to what he could achieve.

Once he was involved in his new project of writing the Brief Lives, Aubrey seems to have stopped work on the Life of Hobbes, but although he never completed it, he wrote the first draft of a Preface (undated; B.L. Hobbes, i, 17–19), in which he explains the origin of his work and defends his method:

> Lectori [To the Reader]
>
> 'Tis religion to performe the will of the dead; which I here discharge, with my promise (1667) to my old friend Mr T.H., in publishing his life and performing the last office to my old friend Mr Thomas Hobbes, whom I have had the honour to know from my child-hood, being his countreyman and borne in Malmesbury hundred and taught my grammar by his school-master.
>
> Since nobody knew so many particulars of his life as myselfe, he was willing that if I survived him, it should be handed to posterity by my

hands, which I declare and avow to doe ingenuously and impartially, to prevent misreports ...

One sayes that when a learned man dyes, a great deal of learning dyes with him. He was a '*flumen ingenii*' ['a stream of genius'], never dry. The *recrementa* [the remains] of so learned a person are valueable. Amongst innumerable observables of him which had deserved to be sett downe, these few (that have not scap't my memory) I humbly offer to the present age and posterity, *tamquam tabulata naufragii* [like planks from a ship-wreck], and as plankes and lighter things swimme, and are preserved, where the more weighty sinke and are lost; and as with the light after sun-sett – at which time clear; by and by the *crepusculum* [twilight]; then total darkness – in like manner is it with matters of antiquitie. Men thinke, because every body remembers a memorable accident shortly after 'tis donne, 'twill never be forgotten, which for want of registring, at last, is drowned in oblivion. Which reflection haz been a hint, that by my meanes many antiquities have been reskued and preserved (I myselfe now inclin-ing to be ancient) – or els utterly lost and forgotten.

For that I am so minute, I declare I never intended it, but setting down in my first draught every particular (with purpose upon review, to re-trench what was superfluous and triviall), I shewed it so some friends of mine (who were also of Mr Hobbes's acquaintance) whose judgements I much value, who gave their opinion: and 'twas clearly their judgement to let ALL stand; for though to some at present it might appear too triviall; yet hereafter 'twould not be scorned but passe for antiquity ...

Like everything else that Aubrey wrote, the Life of Hobbes is unfinished and, despite the high hopes with which he had embarked on the project, it was never published. It contains passages of splendid writing and many of the vivid touches and unique turns of phrase which characterise the best of the *Brief Lives*, but before the end it degenerates into disjointed notes, not worked into the texture of the narrative. Aubrey's mind was always teeming with ideas and he repeatedly moved on to some new project before completing the previous one. He was employed on the *Brief Lives* for the next year fairly intensively and he went on immediately to revise and transcribe other works, hoping to make them ready for publication before he died, and he also started several new works. He never returned to Hobbes.

Chapter XI

The Brief Lives 1680–81

Aubrey was still collecting material for his life of Hobbes at the same time as embarking on his new venture in biography:

London Feb.21,1680

My Singular good Friend!

I received your kind letter of 17 instant, and return you my heartie thankes for your carefull perusall and these excellent Additions there inserted.

Pray before you go to Weston, search for the Moneth and Day of Mr T.H.'s Matriculation. I wish you could see in the Buttery-booke the day that he was entered there. At Trin. Coll. we writ our names in the Buttery-booke when we were entered.

I doubt not to get the honour and favour of the Earl of Dorset (my good friend) (Charles Sackville) to write some verses. Sir W.P[etty] will speake to Edm. Waller and Mr J. Dryden.

It came into my mind Sunday last taking a pipe of tobacco in my chamber (my hand now being-in) to write my honoured friend Sir W. Petty's life, which will be a fine thing, and which he shall peruse himselfe, and then it shall be left among your papers, for Posterity to read (published). I lodged 5 yeares since with Mr Ashmole a sheet of minutes of Jo Dee, who was my great grandfather's great acquaintance and cosen; of Lord Bacon, neer 2 sheets, untouch't by any one: Sir Chr Wren, Mr Robert Hooke, Dr W. Aubrey aforesayd: John Pell D.D ... Richard Boyle, the first Earle of Corke. (Ballard 14, 127)

The verses which he was asking leading poets to supply would have formed an introduction to his Life of Hobbes. Of all his friends in the Royal Society those he admired most were Petty ('whose understanding Genius moves like a Meteor above the sphere of other Mortals' (F39, 275; 23 June 1674)) and Hooke ('He is certainly the greatest mechanick this day in the world' B.L. Hooke). Petty's Life was the first he wrote and one of the fullest.

On 24 February Aubrey suffered a fainting fit, brought on perhaps by the frantic activity of the last two months; he was aged only fifty-four but he seems to have believed that his death was imminent, for prefixed to the first volume of Brief Lives is a note written the same day, in the form of a last will and testament. He recovered quickly enough, for he was soon back at work. The 'will' in which Aubrey leaves his Minutes of Lives to Wood is written on the second folio of Part 1; it is significant since it appears to give Wood some kind of proprietary right in the manuscript:

> *Tamquam tabulata naufragii* [like fragments from a ship-wreck]
> *Sum Johannis Aubrii, R.S.S.* [I belong to, i.e. this is the writing of John Aubrey, Fellow of the Royal Society].
>
> Feb.24, 1680
>
> My will and humble desire is that these minutes, which I have hastily and scriblingly here sett downe, be delivered carefully to my deare and honoured friend Mr Anthony Wood, antiquary, of Oxford.
> *Ita obnixe obtestor* [so I earnestly beseech],
>
> Jo Aubrey
> *Ascensione Domini,*
> *correptus lipothymia, circiter* 3 p.m., 1680 [on Ascension Day, after being seized by a fainting fit at about 3 p.m.] (A6, 2)

The very same day Wood wrote warning him of the risks he might incur if he overstepped the mark in his attack on Fell: 'I sent to Mr Aubrey to have a care what he does if he hath any hand in it – that he must write fair things, or else some body will be on his back' (L & T ii, 480; 24 February 1680). In Aubrey's reply we find the first note of dissatisfaction with Blackburne's efforts; this was to develop into a controversy on the very nature and purpose of biography:

> London, March 7, 1680
>
> Dear Friend!
>
> I cannot enough thanke you for the Care you take of me ... The Doctor [Blackburne] will doe you Right; I did not thinke he could have writt such a delicate Style: 'tis as if Mr Hobbes' Soule were come into his body. But the Doctor is a great judge and consequently magisterial: he is much against Minutiae, which you and Sir Wm Petty would have to stand ...
> Now I am in the writing vaine, perhaps I may venture to complete Malmsebury, Chippenham and Damerham Hundreds, with the records of the Tower. I can annex it to my *Monumenta Britannica* (which I formerly called *Templa Druidum*).
>
> Vivas et valeas, Jo Albericus. (Tanner 456a, 23)

Not content with undertaking his Lives, in his present euphoria he contemplates expanding his work on Wiltshire antiquities and adding to *Monumenta Britannica.*

Three weeks later Blackburne was halfway through his Latin version and it was in a very different style from what Aubrey had intended. But Aubrey was so engrossed in his Lives that although he disapproved of Blackburne's performance and regretted that he himself would get no credit, his spirits were still high. He wrote to Wood:

London, March 27, 1680

My good Friend!

I thanke you heartily for your care in my business concerning the compleating of Mr Hobbes Life ... Dr Blackbourne haz more then half donne, and will doe you Right, and for his style, Mr Dryden (the poet laureate) and my Lord Jo Vaughan much approve of it; but for the compiling, they two agree to leave out all minute things; there will be the trueth, but not the whole. They will not mention his being a Page. Sir W. Petty perused my Copie all over and would have (as also AW) all stand. But I must submit to these great Wits; but in the meantime I suffer the grasse to be cutt under my feet; for Dr Blackbourne will have all the Glory. 'Tis writt in a high style. Now I say the Offices of a Panegyrist and a Historian are much different. A Life is a short History and there the Minuteness of a famous person is gratefull. I never yet knew a Witt (unless he were a piece of an Antiquary) write a proper Epitaph, but leave the reader ignorant, what countryman etc: and only tickles his eares with Elegies [= eulogies] ...

I have to my Booke of Lives made a Kalendar [i.e. an index] of 55 persons, and have donne 10 of them: 3 or 4 leaves a folio a piece. Pray doe your own selfe, though I have you in W. 'Twill be a pretty thing, and I am glad you put me on it. I doe it playingly. This morning being up by ten, I writt two lives: one was Sir John Suckling of whom I wrote a leafe and a halfe in folio.

Could I rise by 7, I could in a moneth write out my booke (2 quires) of Lives: which I will deposite in your handes: as also my Life of Mr Hobbes; I hope the Doctor will restore my papers for me to copie, though he desires to keep those he haz ...

My most humble services to Mr Sheldon when you see him. George Ent was wont to say, a pox take Parties; I say so of Plotters: doe I not well remember the folly of the Cavaliers in their severall senseless plotts against a formed Army? Did they not still more irrctiate themselves, and make their condition worse? even so, even so. Now another plott is started, thought to be of more moment then any yet projected. Too long here to insert. You will quickly hear of it. *Da pacem in diebus nostris, Domine* [Give peace in our days, o Lord].

I have writt memorandums of Sr Walter Raleigh 4 leaves: not yet toucht by any one, for I meddle not with any Memorandum that is already printed; as much of my old friend Dr W. Harvey, never yet touch't. I could afford to putt in Dr Kettle [President of Trinity in Aubrey's time there], though no writer, yet a good man and a good Governour. (Ballard 14, 131)

From this letter it is clear that Aubrey intended to include only writers

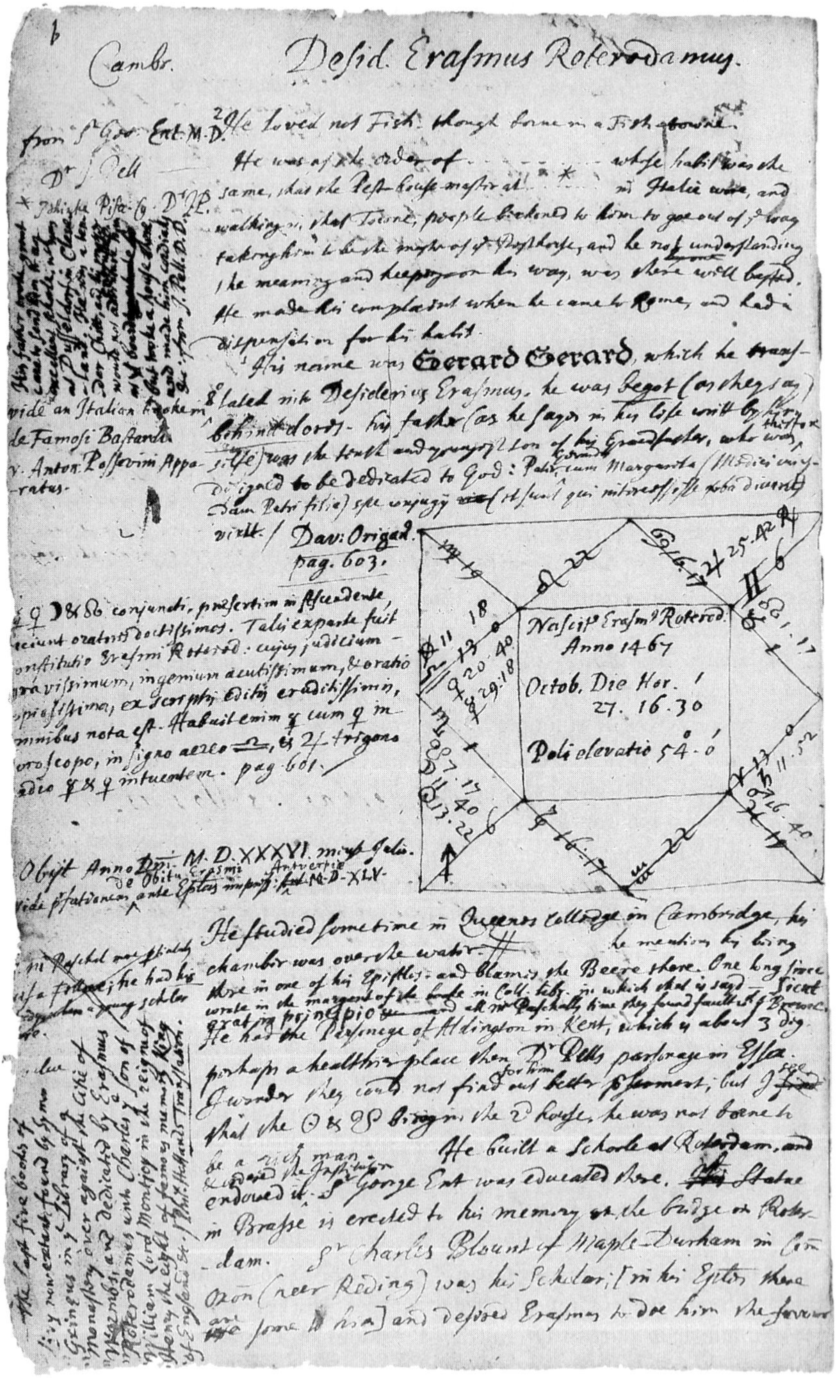
Camb.

Desid. Erasmus Roterodamus.

He loved not Fish, though borne in a Fish-towne.

His name was Gerard Gerard, which he translated into Desiderius Erasmus. he was begot (as they say) behind dores.

Dav: Origan. pag. 603.

Nascit. Erasm. Roterod. Anno 1467 Octob. Die 27. Hor. 16.30 Poli elevatio 54.0

He studied some time in Queens College in Cambridge, his chamber was over the water.

He had the Parsonage of Aldington in Kent, which is about 3 dayes ... perhaps a healthier place than Dr Pells parsonage in Essex. I wonder they could not find out better preferment for him, but I see that the ☉ & ☊ being in the 2d house, he was not borne to be a rich man.

He built a Schoole at Rotterdam, and endowed it. Sr George Ent was educated there. His Statue in Brasse is erected to his memory on the bridge at Rotterdam. Sr Charles Blount of Maple-Durham in Com. Oxon (neer Reding) was his Scholar; [in his Epistles there are some to him] and desired Erasmus to doe him the favour

A page from the manuscript of Aubrey's Brief Lives *(A6, fol. 5v) containing the life of Erasmus. By Kind permission of the Bodleian Library*

in his *Brief Lives* and that he claimed originality for all that he wrote; his material came either first hand from friends or from reports given him by those who had known his subjects. The plot which so concerned him, despite his ususal indifference to political events, may be connected with the machinations of Shaftesbury and Monmouth, who had returned from exile against the King's orders and was making a triumphal tour through the West Country.

Meanwhile he continued to write Lives at a formidable speed; by May the score was sixty-six:

London, May 22, 1680

Dear Friend!

I have received your kind letter of April 19, which I have inserted into my Memoires of Lives (66), a booke of 2 quires close written, and after I had begun it, I had such an impulse of spirit that I could not be quiet till I had donne it.

I have lately been very ill of a cold, and being one day taken with a Lipothymia, fainting away, as soon as I came to myselfe, in the first leaf of the Booke aforesayd, I writt that my Will and humble request was, that these Minutes should be safely transferred to you. They are fine things, but few fitt to be printed in my life or yours …

This afternoon I shall see the proofe of the first sheet of Mr Hobbes his Life [i.e. Blackburne's Latin Life] … Pox take your Orators and Poets; they spoile Lives and histories. The Dr says I am too minute: but a hundred yeare hence that minuteness will be gratefull. Sir Wm Petty ordered me to doe so. He (Blackbourne) would putt it in the High Style … The next thing I shall goe about shall be to transcribe my *Monumenta Britannica* faire, and print it, with my *Chronographia Antiquaria.* (F39, 340)

In June, thinking perhaps that he had finished his work in biography, Aubrey wrote to Wood a formal letter of introduction to the 'Minutes of Lives':

To my worthy friend Mr ANTHONIE WOOD, Antiquarie of Oxford.

London, June 15,1680

Sir!

I have, according to your desire, putt in writing these minutes of lives tumultuarily, as they occurr'd to my thoughts or as occasionally I had information of them. They may easily be reduced to order at your leisure by numbring them with red figures, according to time and place, etc. 'Tis a taske that I never thought to have undertaken till you imposed it upon me, sayeing that I was fitt for it by reason of my generall acquaintance, having not only lived above halfe a centurie of yeares in the world, but have also been much tumbled up and downe in it which hath made me much knowne; besides the modern advantage of coffee-howses in this great citie, before which men knew not how to be acquainted, but with their owne relations, or societies. I might add that I come of a longaevous race, by which means I have imped some feathers from the wings of time, for severall generations; which does reach high. When I first began, I did not thinke I could have drawne it out to so long a thread.

I here lay-downe to you (out of the conjunct friendship between us) the trueth, and, as neer as I can and that religiously as a poenitent to his confessor, nothing but the trueth: the naked and plaine trueth, which is here exposed so bare that the very pudenda are not covered, and affords many passages that would raise a blush on a young maiden's cheekes. So after your perusall, I must desire you to make a castration and to sowe-on some fig-leaves – i.e. to be my Index expurgatorius.

What uncertainty do we find in printed histories, they either treading too neer on the heels of trueth that they dare not speake plaine, or els for want of intelligence (things being antiquated) become too obscure and darke! I doe not here repeat any thing already published (to the best of my remembrance) and I fancy myselfe all along discourseing with you; alledgeing those of my relations and acquaintance (as either you knew or have heard of) *ad faciendam fidem* [as supporting evidence]: so that you make me to renew my acquaintance with my old and deceased friends, and to *rejuvenescere* [grow young again] (as it were), which is the pleasure of old men. 'Tis pity such minutes had not been taken 100 yeares ago: for want wherof many worthy men's names and notions are swallowd-up in oblivion; as much of these also would, had it not been through your instigation: and perhaps this is one of the usefullest pieces that I have scribbled.

I remember one sayeing of generall Lambert's, that 'the best of men are but men at the best': of this, you will meet divers examples in this rude and hastie collection. Now these arcana [secrets] are not fitt to lett flie abroad, till about 30 yeares hence; for the author and the persons (like medlars) ought to be first rotten. But in whose hands must they be deposited in the mean time? advise me, who am, Sir,

Your very affectionate friend
to serve you,
John Aubrey. (A6, 12)

In this letter Aubrey asserts the truth, originality, and importance of his work in biography, and explains why he was peculiarly well suited for the task he had set himself; 'perhaps this is one of the usefullest pieces that I have scribbled', since it helped to save the past, and present, from oblivion. He says that it was at Wood's instigation that he undertook the work and that 'I fancy my selfe all along discourseing with you'; this explains the informal and colloquial style in which much of the Lives is written and the occasional asides addressed to Wood (e.g. 'Quaere if you can find of what howse the famous Owen Glendower was'). In passing, he remarks on the usefulness of coffee houses as a venue for gathering information; these were an important feature of social life, where men of all types gathered to exchange news and gossip; the first was opened at Oxford in 1650 and by 1700 there were over 2,000 of them in London. Aubrey's sociable disposition made him particularly fond of the coffee house; Hooke's diary shows him in the company of his friends of the Royal Society night after night at Garraways or Jonathans.

He did not send the manuscript to Wood in June but continued to enlarge it, until by September its size had almost doubled:

London, Sept.8,1680

Mr Wood,

I received yours of Aug.16 and thought long ere this to have answered it and to have sent together with my Booke of lives; but I have found more matter come-in upon me, so that I have yet about 16 more Lives to write; they will be in all about six score, and I believe never any in England were delivered so faithfully and with so much good authority ... Mr T. Hobb's life will be printed, and out, next weeke; I will send you half a dozen copies. Dr Blackburne haz donne YOU right, but I could not govern him as well as I wish't. He hath not so religiously observed two or 3 passages, as you may see ...

I will send you my Minutes of Lives by, or before, Michaelmas, which 50 yeares hence will be a rarity worth its weight in gold.

Vivas et valeas, J.A. (F39, 347)

It was not until the beginning of November that he sent the promised copy of Blackburne's Life but still did not send his own Minutes of Lives, which were now in the hands of Dr Pell, from whom Aubrey hoped to receive corrections and additions:

London, Nov.3,1680

Mr Wood!

Long lookt for, come at last. I have here sent you Mr Hobbes's Life; and I would have sent you one or two more, as I did intend; but I have but halfe a dozen in all, which was all I had for my paynes; and the Doctor tells me that he had no more. But I doubt – our agreement was that what Mr Crooke gave him, I should have halfe: but he sayes as aforesed, only 6 copies. Be it how it will – he is careless with my papers and keepes them not cleane. I desired him to keepe very clean and carefully the leaf you cutt out of your Booke (which was a great favour): he sent it to the Presse, and there 'tis spoiled. He will shortly doe it into English; and more large. But I will one of these dayes send you one of my owne writing, which you may keep among your papers. I could not govern him, but he has donne it into very good Latin.

Let me knowe how long you stay at Weston, because I shall shortly send you my Collection of Lives, viz. about 100 or more. It is now in Dr Pell's hands. I doe these things with wonderfull ease; and scarce a day, but in my conversations I pick-up some remarque. (F39, 350)

Aubrey was finally disillusioned with Blackburne, who began as such a paragon in his eyes. He had indeed treated him very shabbily; Aubrey had provided all the material, but in his Preface Blackburne mentions him only as one of the friends of Hobbes who had helped him; he describes him with unconscious irony as '*Vir Publico Bono magis quam suo natus* [A man born more for the public good than his own], who chiefly encouraged me to the undertaking of this work, and kindly supplied me with materials'. It is not unfair to say of Blackburne's behaviour what Aubrey had said of Thomas Gore's: 'He hath perused my manuscripts and haz done his businesse, and now a fart for me.'

Wood had still not received the Lives from Aubrey in December and he needed them for his own purposes; returning to Oxford from Weston, he wrote:

Dec.8, 1680

Mr Aubrey,

This is to let you know that I am now in Oxon and therefore if you at any time send your Lives, I shall be at leisure to peruse them, notwithstanding I would have you go on with others in the meane time and let nothing slip your memory, for 'tis my opinion (as of others) that your excellencies lie that way. (F45, 181)

Wood was hard at work on *Athenae Oxonienses*, and Aubrey's Memoirs, which he often paraphrases or even quotes verbatim, were a gift to him. He was bombarding Aubrey with queries, which the latter conscientiously answered; but Aubrey was still unwilling to part with his Lives, which he at last recovered from Dr Pell in January (1681). Pell, old and living in poverty, had proved no help, as Aubrey told Wood in a letter of 13 January:

I deposited my minutes of Lives in Dr Pell's hands in October (or Sept.) expecting he would have made additions and emendments, but (poor disconsolate man) I received it of him without any. So about Candlemas (February 2) next I will send you about 120 Remarques of Lives.

God grant us Peace. I think upon honest G. Ent's sayeing 'A pox on parties!' ...

Tell me I wonder what the Academiques say at the Coffee-houses of Mr Hobbes's Life. The mischief of it is that the great concern of the

> present Politiques do draw away and take the venom of my sting as to the right reverend J.F(ell), as a fitt of the stone diverts the paine from Gowte. I suppose you heare that Dr Tong is dead. (F39, 351)

Dr Ezreel Tonge was Oates's accomplice in the Popish plot. The political turmoil which inspired Aubrey to pray for peace and diverted attention from the Life of Hobbes was caused by the attacks of the Whigs led by Shaftesbury on Charles, and in particular by the bill to exclude the Catholic James Duke of York from the succession. On this issue Charles refused to compromise. He had dissolved Parliament on 20 January and called a new one to meet at Oxford on 21 March. By the time Aubrey wrote again to Wood Parliament had gathered at Oxford, which was now so crowded that Aubrey would not go there at Sir James Long's invitation; Long was anxious to have Aubrey's company at a crisis which he thought would settle the fate of the monarchy, but Aubrey had no wish to be involved in politics even at a distance:

> London, March 19, 1681
>
> Deare Friend!
>
> I heartily entreat your pardon for my long silence, though you are dayly in my thoughts. I will next weeke buckle to finish my Lives for you, which in a weeke I can do. But pray let me know how it may be safely conveyed to you and by whom ... for if it is lost, there is no retrieving it. I might have sent it down by Mr Newman, but 'twas not finish't: neither have I lookt on it since Michaelmas, having only not ill spent my time in reading French Romances, to rub up my French, which was almost growne rusty through desuetude ...
>
> Sir James Long has invited me and is very earnest to have me come to Oxon, but the Towne is so stowed that one must lie by the fireside ...
>
> If I had but either one to come to me in the morning with a good scourge, or did not sitt-up till one or two in the morning with Mr Wyld, I could do a good deale of businesse. I am well pleased in the taske you putt upon me, and Dr Blackburne would have me continue it. (Ballard 14, 129)

Aubrey says that he has not 'lookt on it since Michlemas'; the manuscript was in the hands of Dr Pell from October till January, and during this period Aubrey seems to have taken a holiday from writing, devoting his time to French romances when he was not drinking with Wyld. But he was continuing to collect material which he intended to insert later: 'Scarce a day, but in my conversations I pick-up some remarque' (F39, 350; 3 November 1680).

Receiving no answer from Wood, Aubrey wrote with some asperity: 'What a Gods name, are you asleep, or dead, or what is become of you? I wrote a letter or two to you not long since ... (F39, 358; 2 April

1681). To this Wood replied promptly: 'I have now received two letters from you … My deafness proceeds from a cold moist head and a cold moist stomach, which causes onlie noises, and if the noises were gone, I could heare as well as any (there follows a list of eight queries)' (5 April 1681)

It was June before Aubrey at last let the Minutes of Lives (Parts 1 and 2) out of his hands, when Wood's pretty niece, for whom he had a soft spot, came to collect them:

London, June 21, 1681

Deare Friend,

Long look't for (I hope) is come at last, viz. last day night by your prettie Niece; for whose goodness and Graces the Heavens (I presume) have a blessing in store: I could enlarge: but you expect from me Antiquities and not Complements and amorous Elegies; but pray present my service and Thankes to her.

I have a great many more things to insert but had not time, as also 10 Lives more, and then I thinke I shall trouble you no more …(seven pages of answers to queries and a recipe for deafness provided by Wyld)

Now to your letter of Easter Tuesday – you may keepe my Collection of Lives as long as you please; I will lay aside some sheetes of paper for Continuances or additions etc.

You know I love you heartily and shall be glad to serve you for your owne sake and the worke's sake, without putting you to charges, though I confess I long to see you at Oxon …

Hey ho! 'tis nought but mirth
That keepes the body from the earth … (F39, 354)

Wood must have written an enthusiastic letter of thanks on receiving the Minutes of Lives, for Aubrey replied on 28 June:

London, Vigil of St Pet. & Pauli [= 28 June], 1681

Worthy Friend!

I received your very kind letter last night. I am glad my Memoires pleased you so well. 'Tis pitty they should be buried in Oblivion. I intend to lay papers by me for the future. I have a great deal of Stuff yet remayning, and will shortly send it to you. You may see in my Addresse to you, that I chiefly designe them to be conserved by you, i.e. if you survive me. But it is not fitt for all the Lives to be perused by very few besides your self, because I speake too much truthe, of some that are yet alive: *veritas odium parit* [Truth begets hatred]. You see the papers are altogether rude, indigested, and impolished, and many things frivolous, which I may tell you as my friend, that are not fitt to be published. But as it is, you see it in its *puris naturalibus* [pure natural state, i.e. naked], which pleases an

Antiquary more then to have had it fuscated [i.e. falsely coloured] ... (F39, 397)

The same day Wood wrote sending him a 'Token', for which Aubrey replied thanking him:

London, July 14,1681

Mr Wood!

In answer to yours of 28 of June, I doe give you my thankes for your kind Token, which I received of your brother; which I take very kindly, and shall not forget some time or other (I hope) to requite, *sed fiat Voluntas Domini* [But the Lord's Will be done] ...

I doe earnestly desire you not to lett my MSS of Lives to goe out of your hands; for there is a Scandalum Magnatum (= Scandal against Great Men – an indictable offence), and severe touches of the Earl of Corke, Dr Wallis etc.: that I should heap coales of fire on my head.

About a fortnight hence, I hope to be so happy as to see Oxfordshire. I am invited by my Lord Norreys (who married my Kinswoman), who I hope may give me a lift to some preferment ... (F39, 360)

Aubrey repeatedly warned Wood not to let the Lives out of his hands; his fears were rational enough. James Bertie, Lord Norris, later Earl of Abingdon, had married a daughter of Henry Danvers and so was distantly related to Aubrey by marriage. After the death of Thanet in 1679, he became his chief patron and treated him with great kindness, often inviting him to his houses at Lavington near Devizes and Ryecote near Oxford.

When Aubrey sent Wood the manuscript of his Lives in June, he wrote as if this project was nearly completed, but by September he was at it again, planning to insert a mass of new material and to write the lives of the English poets:

London September 1st 1681

Deare Friend,

I must beg pardon that I have been so long silent. I intend (God willing) about the middle of this moneth to be at Oxon or Ricot. If you are at Oxon, let me know how long you stay there: for I have collected (*in adversariis* [in note books]) about quier of good matter, which I would bring along with me did I know I should spend 4 or 5 dayes with you. I long to be with you; I have lost severall friends lately, amongst others my brother Tom, dyed a fortnight since.

Did I tell you that I mett with old Mr Beeston who knew all the old English poets, whose lives I am taking from him? His father was master of the ... playhouse. Seeing the uncertainty of life, and how few there are

> that transmitt memoires to posterity, it make me more eager to persue what I have begun. (F39, 357)

Tom had lived at Broad Chalke and ran the farm there; he died suddenly on 15 August. On Tom's death, William moved into Broad Chalke; Aubrey had never got on well with William and this move was to cause endless trouble later.

Unfortunately old William Beeston died before Aubrey had learnt much from him, and so a great opportunity was missed. Dryden decribed Beeston as 'the Chronicle of the Stage', and Aubrey made a note: 'William Shakespeare – *quaere* Mr Beeston, who knowes most of him'. But Aubrey was too late; the Life of Shakespeare is very thin and only one important note is attributed to Beeston: 'Though, as Ben Johnson sayes of him, that he had but little Latine and lesse Greek, he understood Latine pretty well, for he had been in his younger yeares a schoolmaster in the country – from Mr Beeston.' This statement, made on such good authority, should surely be accepted.

We cannot tell what Part 2 of Brief Lives (A7) contained. When Aubrey got it back from Wood in 1692, he found that Wood had cut out pages 1–44, including the Index; only two folios of the original manuscript survive (see page 140).

In September 1681 Aubrey visited Oxford and while he was there gave Wood Part 3 (A8); this is headed:

> Auctarium vitarum a JA collectarum, anno Domini 1681 [Supplement to the Lives collected by JA A.D.1681] ...
>
> For Mr Anthony Wood
> at
> Oxford.

It consists of four leaves for an Index followed by thirty-eight folios of Lives, including many notes which correct or add to earlier Lives. Aubrey recalled this to make additions a month later ('pray send up by your Brother the Auctarium I gave you, to be more compleat' (Tanner 456a, 27; 22 October 1681). Pasted on the title page is a slip written by Wood, asking Aubrey to let him have it back:

> Mr Aubrey,
>
> I beseech you as you have been civill in giving this book to me at Oxon in Sept.1681, so I hope when you have done with it, you'l returne every part of it againe to your servant,
>
> Ant.Wood. 11 Nov.1681

Aubrey returned it to Wood in May the following year.

Bound up with this part is the plan for another biographical treatise which Aubrey intended to put together later: 'An Apparatus for the lives of our English mathematical written by Mr John Aubrey, R.S.S., March 15, 1690.' This, which remained unfinished, consists of thirty-three folio pages.

In all Aubrey composed 426 lives, differing in length from a few words (e.g. on John Holywood he wrote only: 'Dr Pell is positive that his name was Holybushe') to four full folios (e.g. Petty and Francis Potter). Aubrey acknowledged the disorderly state of the manuscript he sent to Wood; the Lives were written 'tumultuarily as they occurred to my thoughts or as I occasionally received information of them'; they would need editing.

Most of the more important Lives were written between February 1680 and September of the following year. It had been a period of high spirits and continuous creative activity apart from a break of five months (October 1680-March 1681), when, according to his own report he devoted his time to reading French romances and debauching with Wyld. He had thoroughly enjoyed his incursion into biography, discovering a talent he had not been conscious of and writing with great facility ('I doe these things with wonderfull ease'). In none of the letters of this time is there any hint of the lethargy or melancholy to which he was so often subject.

Aubrey sent the manuscript of the Lives to Tanner in June 1693 to be deposited in the Ashmolean in the personal custody of Edward Llwyd (see page 144). It lay there concealed from public view until almost exactly a hundred years later the Shakespearian scholar Edward Malone transcribed most of the Lives for publication (1792), but this project came to nothing. The first complete and accurate text of the Lives was that of Andrew Clark (Oxford, 1898). This scholarly edition included everything apart from a few short passages which Clark considered obscene, but it was not intended for popular consumption; Clark's purpose, as he states in his introduction (page 6) was that 'the entire contents of these MSS will be placed beyond the risk of perishing ... and that they will henceforth be accessible to all'. The first popular edition was the selection edited by John Collier and called *The Scandal and Credulities of John Aubrey* (London, 1931), a title which reflects the estimation placed on Aubrey at this time. This was followed by Anthony Powell's *Brief Lives* in 1949, and in the same year by Oliver Lawson Dick's edition; the latter was the first edition in a readable form which is almost complete.

In the letter Aubrey wrote to Wood as the Preface to the Lives, he says: 'Tis pity that such minutes had not been taken 100 yeares since or more: for want wherof many worthy men's names and notions are swallowed-up in oblivion; as much of these also would <have been>, had it not been through your instigation; and perhaps this is one of the usefullest pieces that I have scribbled.'

Ever since as an undergraduate he had commissioned the drawings of Osney Abbey, he had considered that one of his most important functions in life was to preserve the past from being swallowed up in oblivion, a fate which overhung all human events and persons: 'And as with the light after sun-sett – at which time, clear; by and by comes the crepusculum (twilight), then total darkness – in like manner is it with matters of antiquitie' (letter to the Reader, prefacing the Life of Hobbes). In preserving for posterity accounts of both great figures from the past and eminent contemporaries, he was adding to the sum of human knowledge, and in performing this valuable function, he was determined to write not panegyric but the 'naked and plaine truth', including minutiae which the more conventional biographers of his time rejected.

But he achieved much more than mere recording; he had the painter's eye which enabled him to recreate those of whom he wrote in the mind of his readers in vivid detail, and an outstanding literary talent, which unfailingly supplied him with the telling phrase. In the Preface to the *Wiltshire Antiquities* he says: 'The retrieving of these forgotten things from Oblivion in some sort resembles the Art of the Conjurer, who makes those walke and appeare that have been lodged in their graves many hundreds of yeares: and to represent as it were to the eie, the places, Customes, and Fashions that were of old Times.' For us, living 300 years after Aubrey, he is such a conjurer whose magic seldom fails to surprise and delight.

Chapter XII

'We must not lose TIME' 1681–85

AFTER RETURNING FROM THE VISIT TO OXFORD at which he gave Wood Part 3 of the Lives, Aubrey wrote a letter of thanks:

London, Oct.22,1681

Dear Friend!

I returne you my heartie Thankes for your Civilities to me at Oxon ... I cannot expresse what a wonderfull refreshing 'twas to my Soule to spend a week at Oxon among so many good and ingeniose acquaintances. Besides I owe adoration to the very Buildings and Groves and am ready almost to offer sacrifice, methinkes, when I there doe *rejuvenescere* [grow young again]. Pray send me up by your Brother the Auctuarium I gave you to be more compleat. (Tanner 456a, 27)

His love of Oxford was unfailing; he had a wide circle of friends there and it was their 'ingeniose conversation' which he enjoyed above all things. It may therefore seem surprising that when there appeared to be an opportunity to move to Oxford and at the same time achieve a profitable preferment, he hesitated to take it. For in December he wrote to Wood:

London, Dec.20, 1681

Mr Wood,

Last night I found a letter in my chamber from my neighbour Sr Jo Saintlowe of Chalke Parish, intimating that Dr Lampshire was dangerously ill, if not dead, and that he would have me adresse my selfe to my friend Mr Secretary Jenkins, to use his interest to procure it for me. Now I say unto you, *tali non sum dignus honore* [I am not worthy of such an honour]. I am an ignote fellow and but of little learning. They will surely choose some worthy man: Dr Plott were a fitt person. Now this proposall is odd. I could not choose but give you animadversion of it, but the Right Reverend Father in God J. Fell Bishop of Oxon would not like it, and I beleeve he influences all in all ... I am beholding to Sr John for his good wishes; but lett me heare from you by the next post without fayle. If I should have it, I should be like a weaned child, to leave Mr Wyld, who are inseparable and dote together till 12 or 1 at night: but I find Dr Crowdon (Principal of St Mary Hall) is a non-resident at Oxon, and if my Lord Norris obtaine it for me, as he is willing and I doubt not (if we have peace) can procure it, that will be worth 2, or 300li per annum, and then I should be able to doe some fine things and doe my friends good too. So much for that.

I have made a Collection of Nativities of learned men, beyond expectation, out of old English Astrologers that lived above a hundred years since, manuscripts which Mr W. Lilly had, and are now in possession of Mr Elias Ashmole. By Aprill, I hope to turn over 40 Volumes ... Mr Ashmole turnes and reads, and I doe write. I will after Xmas goe most Sundayes to him; we turne over a volume in an hower or a little more.

Vivas et valeas, and to Dr Plott,
Tuissimus,
Jo Gregorius.

After the opiating quality of the mince-pies is exhaled, I will begin with old Mr Beeston about the Lives of the Poets. But what comfort have one to doe these things, for which one have generally but scorne and contempt? (Ballard 14, 134)

Dr John Lamphire was Principal of Hart Hall and one of the 'Merry Gang' which was the centre of Aubrey's social life in Oxford. In the event Saintlowe's proposal proved premature, since Lamphire recovered from his illness and continued as Principal until his death in 1688. We see again that to procure such preferment, the key was 'interest'; this time, that of Mr Secretary Jenkins or Lord Norris (later Earl of Abingdon). Aubrey had known Sir Leoline Jenkins for many years, for he was the son of a copyholder of his cousin Sir John Aubrey; he is a classic example of the rewards to be won by talent, irrespective of class; he had gradually risen to become a judge and diplomat and had been appointed Secretary of State the previous year. Aubrey had called on him to congratulate him on his appointment: 'When I came to wayte on him to congratulate for the honor his majestie had been pleased to bestowe on him, he recieved me with his usuall courtesie, and sayd that "it had pleased God to rayse-up a poore worme to doe his majestie humble service"' (B.L. Jenkins). Despite his courtesy, he proved no help to Aubrey, who says in his autobiographical notes: 'I expect preferment [through] Sir L. Jenkins.'

Aubrey is clearly reluctant to enter for the post of Principal of Hart Hall; he shows a modesty which was not evident when he planned to make to Gloucester Hall an 'ingeniose nest' (see page 71). But he was at this time leading a life that suited him, working on his Lives and the *Collectio Geniturarum*, merrymaking with Edmund Wyld, and enjoying the conversation of his friends of the Royal Society; and he was perhaps a little afraid of making so drastic a change in his way of life, unless he could hold the post in absence.

Ashmole had bought Lilly's huge collection of Nativities from his widow and was now dictating parts of it to Aubrey in his house at Lambeth. For Aubrey this was a most welcome addition to his own Collection, which he was continually augmenting.

Mulling over the question of Hart Hall, it suddenly occurred to Aubrey that Wood was the man to be Principal:

London, St Jo Eve-day (27 December), 1681

Dear AW,

I sent you a letter lately in relation to an overture from my neighbour Sr Jo. Saintlowe concerning Dr Lampshire: I wrote it over a glasse of wine upon the receipt of it. I begin now to think that I dote, upon account of 2 late overtures; and both received at the same time and as hastily and inconsiderately answered by the same post. First, as to AW. 'Twas but just now, taking a pipe of Tobacco at my friend E[dmund] W[ild], it occurred to my thoughts, why should not AW be the most fitt person to succeed Dr L[amphire]? When I wrote my letter to you (hand over head), I no more thought of him then of Roger Bacon, or any other learned Clarke dead severall centuryes since. But though you are a man that makes no bustle in the world, nor no boaster, who is there (in merit) who can come into competition with you? If the place is voyd, I will use all my interest with Secretary Jenkins for you: and which is more, I will write speedily to my singular good friend Sr Wm Petty in Dublin, to whom the Duke of Ormond will deny nothing. Your name and character **from his mouth** is recommendation enough: and though I might be sure of the place (for which I am altogether, I confesse, unfitt) I would have that deference and respect for AW that hath done such service to the University, that I would make an oblation of it to him.

My other dotage was this: I was that night enform'd of a Bargaine of an estate to be had ... But of this, not a word.

Vivas et valeas,
Tuissimus, J.A. (Ballard 14, 135)

Aubrey is singularly unrealistic in offering to make an 'oblation' of Hart Hall to Wood; the latter's reputation as a crypto-Catholic would surely have been a bar, apart from the fact that he had by now quarrelled with most of the influential men at Oxford. And his interest in 'a Bargaine of an estate' is fantastical at a time when he was having to sell his books to make ends meet.

Three months passed before he wrote again to say that he was going to send Wood a quire of papers; this was a revision of the third part of *Brief Lives*:

London, Easter Eve (15 April), 1682

My worthy and honoured Friend!

In the first place I beg your pardon for my long silence but hope I shall make a good and acceptable returne. I desire you to send me a letter by the next post to let me know whether you are alive, and, if so, at Oxon: because I would not have my Collections miscarry. If I heare from you, expect then in a weeke's time my sending you my papers (a quier) …

I wish you a merry Easter and am zealously

Your affectionate and ready friend to serve you,
J.A.

Now the warm weather comes on, I growe exceedingly active and begin to consider that we are all mortall men, and that we must not lose TIME. (A12, 8)

It was May before he got round to sending back to Wood the third part of the Lives, as we learn from a letter in which he answers Wood's queries and complains of William's behaviour. William was now living at Broad Chalke, running the farm. Relations between the brothers were deteriorating fast:

London, May 11,1682

Worthy Friend!

Yesterday I delivered my 3d Volume together with a Booke of Mr Hobbes, which Dr Blackburne gives you … I wish you could send to Mr Kelsey of Newton Tony; I lay at his house two severall nights and was civilly entertained: I frankely and heartily promised to send him some venison and spake to my brother accordingly (for at Chalke you must know that we have the command of venison enough). The Divil a Buck's foot did they ever send to him; neither did I ever receive a piece of venison here to oblige a friend. Be so that, I suspect he is disobliged, thinking that I did shamme him with what I never intended … I writt to my brother William, who is now at Kington St Michael, to see the Christian name of White [John White, bishop of Winchester, d.1560?] and [his] obiit [i.e. year of death], which he may doe with a wett finger, if he will. I have Mars in the 3rd House, which shewes I should never receive any good from my relations; the neerer the worse.

Tuissimus,
Jo Albericus.

When I come to Oxon, I might make Castration in my first part (of *Brief Lives*); for besides Scandalum Magnatum, there be other things too reflecting on others. (F39, 362)

Wood was now hard at work on *Athenae Oxonienses* and flooding Aubrey with queries, often asking for information which Aubrey had already supplied, to the latter's irritation: 'I tell you once more ...'; 'surely I gave you the name of ...' On Clarendon he tells Wood: 'His sonne, the present Earl of Clarendon, will shortly give me an Abstract of his Life ... I will in time answer your other Quaeries.' To this he adds in a P.S.:

> I think I told you that this Earl of Clarendon told me his father was writing the History of our late times. He beginnes with King Charles 1st and brought it to the Restauration of King Charles IId. When he was writing, the penne fell out of his hands; he tooke it up again to write; it fell out once more. So then he perceived he was attacqued by the death, sc. the palsey. They say 'tis very well donne, but his sonne will not print it. (F39, 365; 24 June 1682)

The second earl eventually published his father's *History of the Rebellion* in 1704, when the political situation was calmer; he presented it to Oxford University, and from the profits of this work a new printing house was built, the Clarendon Press.

Wood must have been pressing Aubrey to make haste, for in his next letter Aubrey apologises for the delay in answering his queries:

> London, July 26, 1682
>
> Deare Friend,
>
> I hope I have sufficiently fulfilled your desire in answer to all your Queries, but my old friend seigner Wyld hath brought me to the old habit again (they told me he wanted me extremely): he haz made me loose 2 or 3 opportunities of sending those things inclosed to you: but I hope they will come soon enough, and safe ...
>
> Pray keepe my Leviathan [i.e. the Lives] safe, which I much value: next spring I intend to peruse it again.
>
> Tuissimus,
> Jo Albericus. (F39, 368)

In an attempt not to 'lose Time', Aubrey had evidently been avoiding Wyld's company, but now he was back to the 'old habit', making merry with him till the small hours, which left him fit for little the next day.

He sent one more set of answers to Wood's queries in August and then nothing until May the following year, when he wrote apologising for his 'long silence': 'for I have of these late months been taken up with Mundane affairs, and out of humour.' (Ballard 14, 136; 10 May, 1683).

The 'Mundane affairs' which put Aubrey out of humour at this time were probably connected with his quarrel with his brother William. When Tom died in 1681, William had moved into Chalke and took over the farm. Ten years later Aubrey wrote to Wood: 'I am mightily discomposed about my brother; I intrusted him with my estate at Chalke (250li per annum) almost two years' (F39, 411; 4 January 1691). In another letter of 23 October 1688, in which he is telling Wood of the arrangements he has made for the disposal of his manuscripts, he says: 'I sent 4 or 5 years since (upon a threatening of my brother to throw me into Gaole) those things to Mr Ashmole ...' It seems that Aubrey had entrusted William with the estate in 1681 and that when he took it away from him early in 1683, William threatened Aubrey with legal action.

Aubrey did not write to Wood again until January 1684. The cause of this hiatus in their correspondence was Aubrey's lethargy, induced by the death of friends, especially that of George Johnson. Johnson was born the same week as Aubrey and was a near neighbour to him at Easton Piers; they had been at Blandford School together. He studied at the Middle Temple with Aubrey and went on to become a judge of the North Wales circuit and Solicitor to the Treasury. The reversion of the Mastership of the Rolls was granted him in 1667, and he had promised to make Aubrey one of his secretaries when he succeeded to the post, but the incumbent, Sir Harbottle Grimston, outlived him, dying in 1685 at the age of eighty-three.

London, Jan.26, 1684

Dear Friend,

You may well admire that I who have so great a respect for you and your undertakings (to which I so well wish) have been so long silent: and truely I am really ashamed and sorry that I have been so. But (I doe assure you) it proceeds from noe neglect, or forgetfullnesse, for I have my pockets full of Memoires now almost worn out for you these three quarters of a yeare, which I thought to have sent these last two Termes by your Brother and which I intend now by a gent commoner of Corpus Christi.

It pleased God at Whitsontide last to bereave me of a deare, usefull, and faithfull friend (Mr Johnson), who held the reversion of the place of Master of the Rolles: who generously and for friendships and neighbourhoods sake (we were borne in the same week and within four miles, and were educated together) gave me the graunt to be one of his Secretaries, which place is worth 500li per annum. He was a strong lustie man and died of a malignant fever, infected by the Earl of Abingdon's brother, making of his Will. It was such an opportunity, that I shall never see the like again. I should have dispersed the profit, *ad Maiorem Dei Gloriam* [to the greater glory of God]; and been usefull and gratefull, and benefactical to my ingeniose friends: in which ranke A.W. has one of the highest places.

Since then I have lost my learned and good friend Jo Collins [a distinguished mathematician, F.R.S.], whom you knew: and also another, which so discomposed me, that I have been as it were lethargiq ...

I consider my mortality, and therefore intend by Easter-terme to putt all my poore Scribbles into your hands. God blesse you, and all lovers of Antiquity.

Your truly affectionate friend and servant,
Jo Aubrey. (Ballard 14, 137)

If Johnson had lived longer, Aubrey's situation might have been radically improved; his early death was a bitter blow, depriving him of his last realistic hope of gaining preferment. It also reminded him of his own mortality and brought on a depression lasting several months. When he had thrown this off, he got down to revising his manuscripts, especially his *Natural History of Wiltshire* and his *Idea of Education*; the latter was a work he was particularly fond of containing detailed proposals for the reform of education.

In the midst of these scholarly preoccupations, Aubrey embarked on another fruitless attempt to mend his fortunes. In May 1685 Paschall had written to him; he was an old friend, rector of Chedzoy near Bridgwater, who conducted an endless correspondence with Aubrey about the 'Universal Character'; he was in a high state of excitement about a scheme they were hatching to operate some lead mines in the Mendips; they seem to have had three other partners, including Abingdon, who had undertaken to finance the project. Paschall was expecting Aubrey at Chedzoy: 'Pray make all hast you can'. He was already planning how to dispose of the profit from the mines:

One thing I know you will join with me in ... the first ten shares of the clear profits to be consecrated to God, by whose guidance you and I are, I believe, convinced this instance of his Goodness was brought to this passe. I would save it set apart for the promotion of usefull knowledge, particularly in my Country. Who knows but it may serve your Idea [i.e. *The Idea of Education*]? But more of that when we meet. Shall I need to say that you shall be really welcome here? Indeed, my friend, I feel an inexpressible pleasure in the thought of the benefit may accrue hence to you. (A13, 74; 15 May, 1685)

Once again Aubrey must have felt that he was within reach of success, but in the end Abingdon withdrew his support and the project collapsed.

With his extraordinary ability to be at the wrong place at the wrong time, Aubrey arrived at Chedzoy on 11 June; it was the very day

Monmouth landed at Lyme Regis, as he told Wood in a letter of 3 August:

Broad Chalke Aug.3, 1685

Dear Friend,

I went from London Tuesday in Whitsonweeke into Somerset to an ingeniose friend of mine, and came just that night as Monmouth began his Rebellion. It was not without danger that I came hither: Monmouth's soldiers came into my friend's house (Mr Paschal) and tooke away horses and armes and came into my bed chamber as I was abed. But Deo Gratias [thanks be to God!], that Cloud is overblown. Within this fortnight I shall goe thither againe, where I shall be glad to serve you. (F39, 374)

Monmouth landed at Lyme Regis on 11 June and had soon collected a following of 6,000 men. He was proclaimed king at Taunton and then advanced on Bristol. When Bristol would not open its gates to him, he retired to Bridgwater. The government forces encamped at Sedgemoor, a few miles from Bridgwater. On 5 July Monmouth attempted to surprise them in a night attack but after a fierce battle the rebel army was broken and Monmouth fled. When he was captured, he was brought to the house of Aubrey's old Trinity friend, Anthony Ettrick, at this time MP for Christ Church, Hants, who committed him for trial.

Aubrey at this time planned to make Wood his literary executor; he had written to him in January 1674: 'I consider my mortality, and therefore intend by Easter-Terme to put all my poore Scribbles into your hands' (Ballard 14, 137). He had already entrusted him with the task of publishing the Lives after he was dead and now sends him the Wiltshire Antiquities, which some years before he had asked Wood to revise for him.

Aug.17,1685

Mr Wood!

I received yours of the 8th instant. I am exceedingly sorry and troubled for the death of that excellent man Mr Allan: I sent by him to you my two Volumes of Antiquities of Wilts, A and B, of which you make no mention ... I sent them to you that they might not perish: I am much afraid they are lost. My Naturall Historie of Wilts came to Mr Paschall but last weeke: the Box all broken to Splinters, and 'twas sent downe at Whitsontide. We see how apt MSS are to be lost ...

No man would be more gladly willing to serve you at Sarum then my self, but I dare not appear there at present; and the Ecclesiastics are such porei [= porail – weak things] and there are such factions among them, I cannot rely on them: but a little before the Terme, as I goe to London, I will steale one day there as I goe and doe it for you. (F39, 375)

The Antiquities of Wiltshire had in fact arrived safely as Wood tells Aubrey:

> 22 Aug.85
>
> Sir,
>
> I have now received your 2nd letter dated from Broad Chalke for which I thanke you ...Your two books of Wiltshire I received by the hands of Mr Allan the very next day after his returne from London, and therefore trouble yourself no more about the matter. (Tanner 456a, 33)

(Wood's friend Mr Allan died 'of the small pox about 3 weekes after his return from London, to the great resentment of all those who knew the vertue and learning in him' (Wood-Aubrey 8 August 85; F45, 190).

Later Aubrey changed his mind and decided to leave all his papers to the Ashmolean, thinking they would be safer there; Wood was exceedingly angry at this and at first refused to hand the papers over to Plot, the Keeper of the Museum (see pages 114, 117). This dispute prepared the ground for the terrible quarrel which was to flare up some years later.

Chapter XIII

'My Tygre Brother' 1686–89

Aubrey did not go to London the following term but stayed on at Broad Chalke for some months; he may have been settling his mother, who had moved there from Bridgwater earlier in the summer. After their mother's arrival at Chalke there was a furious quarrel between Aubrey and William, which left Aubrey prostrate, as he told Wood the following January:

> London, Jan 2nd 1686
>
> Deare Friend,
>
> I returned hither about St Andrewe's tyde [= 30 November] from Chalke, where my domestick troubles were so great, that I was hardly able to sustayne them: whether ever I shall shake-off the griefe, I know not. If it had not been for those troubles I would have willingly gonne to Salisbury and have answered your Queries. I have not been able to read, or write, these six weekes for griefe; and this is but the 3d letter that I have writt. My Tygre brother and I are at so great a difference (too long here to relate) that I beleeve we shall never close again ...
>
> (Answers to Queries)
>
> I wish you a happy New-Yeare and another such friend (if posible) as Mr Allan. I am Tuissimus,
>
> J.Albericus (F39, 377)

The difference between Aubrey and William will certainly have been on the question of what should happen to Chalke when their mother died – she was now aged seventy-five, her health was poor, and she had probably returned to Chalke to spend her last days with her sons. Broad Chalke Manor Farm formed part of the Wilton estates of Lord Pembroke and had been leased to Aubrey's family since 1601. The lease was of the type called 'pur autre vie', for the duration of three lives. Following Richard Aubrey's death, a lease dated 20 September 1662 was made to 'Deborah Aubrey, widow of Richard, for the lives of Deborah and her two sons John and William'. On her death the lease would revert to Aubrey; as we shall see, Aubrey intended to sell it, and we may surmise that William was opposed to this and was desperately anxious about his own position. Leases *pur autre vie* were so secure that it was not unusual for them to be sold to another party; if the first name in the lease wished to sell against the wishes of the other names, the rights of the latter were open to legal dispute. We shall find that when Aubrey planned to sell the lease to Matthew Kent the following year, William Aubrey challenged the legality of the sale in the chancery courts.

Wood answered Aubrey's outpouring of grief with an extraordinarily unsympathetic and peremptory reply:

Jan.10,86

Mr Aubrey,

I am sorry that things go unluckily between you and your brother, and more sorry that you have done nothing of my queries, and therefore if you have them still by you, pray send them forthwith in your next, but let them be wrapt up so neatly that it may be but a 2nd letter …

Besides the Queries that I sent to you at Salisbury, I sent others in the letter that enclosed them, but you have not made answer to anything …

Yrs A.W. (F45, 192)

In April Deborah Aubrey died at Chalke, her last days saddened by the quarrel between her sons, about which she had told Paschall. Before he had heard of her death Paschall had written to Aubrey:

Just now comes a letter from your good mother. I am sorry to heare of her great illness, and grieve withall. God Almighty be her comfort. She wishes she may leave them friends that ought to be so. I am sure you will do what is requisite on your part toward it. (A13, 77; 20 April 1686)

It was three weeks before Aubrey could bring himself to write to Wood, making no reference to the latter's last ill-natured letter:

London, May 11,1686

Dear Friend,

In January last, after a very great conflict of affliction, I roused up my spirits and writt a letter to you, and immediately fell to worke with my Naturall Historie of Wilts, which I had just donne April 21st, i.e. rough hewn, and finished the last chapter, when at the evening I heard the sad newes of the Decease of my deare and ever honoured Mother: who died at Chalke, but my brother haz buried her with my Father in North Wilts (Kington St Michael). My head haz been a fountain of teares, and this is the first letter (except of businesse) that I have writt since my Griefe.

I am now involved in a great deal of trouble; and Chalke must be sold: but I hope to make some reservation for my selfe; and I hope before I dye to be able to make an honourable present to you. I shall shortly goe to Chalke, to see how matters goe there: and as soon as I can pick up a little money intend to see you at Oxon, and I think the time very long till I am with you ... I shall bring severall memoranda with me to insert. God bless you and comfort me, that I may live to finish and publish my papers ... Let me desire you to write to me by by the next post to let me know how you doe. Your letter will be a cordiall to me ... I must make hast with my papers, for I am now sixty.

Tuissimus, J.A. (Ballard 14, 139)

No letters survive between May and September; probably Aubrey was 'lethargic', in a deep depression brought on by his mother's death and his quarrel with William.

He wrote briefly to Wood on 25 September, sending an epitaph (F39, 380), and then silence again until the following February. In this letter we learn that William is having recourse to law to establish his rights and that Aubrey is overwhelmed by the whole affair but hopes to get back to work as soon as it is settled:

London, Feb.5, 1687

Deare Friend!

You may thinke it much that I have not writt to you this long Time; but this is to acquaint you that I have been so weekely perplext and plagued by letters from my brother; and with running up and downe, to Lawyers and Proctors, that I have had no time to think my owne thoughts, or do any thing for you, or my Naturall History. But as soon as terme ends, I will perform my promise to Sr W. Dugdale, viz. to make fitt for the Presse my *Templa Druidum.* I hope in April to come to Oxford for 3 or 4 dayes: and then I shall putt some things out of my Memorandums into my Collection of Lives. After the Terme, I will doe all that possibly lies in my power for you: and I hope before I die, to present you with an Honorable Token of my love and Friendship to you.

Vivas et valeas, Tuissimus, J.A. (Ballard 14, 141)

The last sentence suggests that Aubrey hoped to have settled the business of the sale of Chalke before the end of the legal term and that he would be left well enough off to make a present to Wood.

For the time being there is no further news of legal proceedings, and in his next letter (28 July, F39, 384) Aubrey tells Wood that he has been invited to visit a friend in Yorkshire, 'as far as Ripon'. He left at the beginning of the next month:

London, Aug.4,1687

Sir,

I am just now taking horse for Yorkshire ... About the end of the month

I intend to be here again, and about a weeke after with you at Oxon. (F39, 398)

This was an exceptionally difficult and depressing time for Aubrey; apart from the death of his mother, his letters record the deaths of several old friends; the quarrel with William and the consequent entanglement with lawyers were draining his energy and he could not get on with his work; he was again being pursued by creditors. Moreover, he had now left his lodgings with Mris More near Gresham College where he had lived for the last ten years (perhaps she had died, or perhaps he had failed to pay his rent); from now on he was perpetually on the move from one unsatisfactory lodging to another.

But the trip to Yorkshire restored his spirits, just as the perambulation of Surrey had done fifteen years earlier. It was a considerable undertaking; it would have taken him several days to ride to Yorkshire and while he was there he got round to many sites of archaeological interest, on which he added notes to his *Monumenta Britannica*, and made observations which he included in a revision of the *Natural History of Wiltshire.*

On his return he was in high spirits and embarking on a new project, 'An Interpretation of Villare Anglicanum', an attempt to explain the meaning of the place names of towns and rivers listed in *Villare Anglicanum* (*A View of the Towns of England*, Spelman and Dodsworth, 1656) by reference to their British (i.e. Celtic) origins. He wrote in October, following a visit to London by Wood:

London, Oct.27,1687

Deare Friend,

I give you my hearty Thankes for your Civil Entertaynments at London, which I shall not forgett ...

I have dipt my finger in inke this month, and about halfe waye oversea: sc. to transcribe all the British names I can find in the *Villare Anglicanum* and to interpret them by the help of Dr Davies Dictionary (which is very imperfect) and with the assistance of some of my Welsh friends, and am under the temptation to doe the like for the old English words out of Whelocks Saxon Dictionary ...

I do not desire Mr A. Wood to keep the papers safe I left with him: being confident of his care in such matters. When I come to Oxford, I shall bring a matter of 3li or more with me and stay there a fortnight, where I hope I shall be out of harmes way, and also I would runne over the marginall notes of Holinsheds *Chronicle* for some naturall philosophicall Remarques for my Naturall Historie of Wilts, which I forgott to shew you; and I am under a temptation since I sawe you, to write Memoires of that kind of Gloucestershire, Monmouthshire, Flyntshire, and Surrey;

having long since pickt up considerable Remarques, many whereof will be utterly lost to posterity without I stitch them together.

Now what shall I say, or doe, with these pretty Collections? I thought to have made Mr R. Hooke my Executor if I dye before I doe it myselfe: but he has so much to doe of his owne that he will not be able to finish. And you know how Dr Plot served me. I shall write them legibly: and if you survive me, you would be more carefull of them than anybody els. Mr Elias Ashmole growes old and sickly. I hope before I die to be able to leave you an Honourable token of my Love and your Friendship: and would have you search the Records for my Antiquities of Wilts, to finish it: and I will endeavour to satisfy you. (F39, 392)

Following this letter there was a year's hiatus in their correspondence. Aubrey had visited Oxford and dined with Wood and Plot at the Mermaid Tavern on 13 June (1688) (L & T, iii, 269); Plot had been appointed Keeper of the new Ashmolean Museum in 1783 (on 17 February 1683 Ashmole wrote in his diary: 'The last load of my rarities was sent to the barge, and this afternoon I relapsed into gout.'). At their meeting Aubrey must have told Wood of his decision to leave all his papers in the Ashmolean and asked him to hand them over to Plot. This decision was occasioned partly by the political situation: James II's attempt to Catholicise England, culminating in the trial of the seven bishops (June 1688), had united all against him, and a wave of anti-Catholic feeling was again sweeping the country; William of Orange had already been secretly invited to intervene and he was to land at Tor Bay on 5 November. Since Wood was suspected of being a Catholic, Aubrey felt that his papers were not safe in his hands during these tumultuous days.

When he next wrote to Wood on 23 October (1688), the euphoria of the previous year had evaporated; his health was poor, he had no permanent lodging, and he was separated from his books. Moreover, he was terrified of how William would behave if he learnt of his plan to sell the lease of Broad Chalke and keep a reservation for himself. He recognises that he has 'injured his poore brother', but attempts to justify his behaviour to himself and to Wood. It is the letter of a man in the depths of black depression: 'My heart is almost broke: and I have much adoe to keep up my poor spirits.' He begins by pressing Wood to hand over his papers to Dr Plot for the Museum; Wood had just received another box of manuscripts from Aubrey but was refusing to surrender anything:

London, Oct.23, 1688

Deare Friend!

I am exceedingly glad that the Boxe is come safely to your hands. I shall now dye with greater peace of mind. On Sunday last I went to Mr Ashmole, who shewed me a letter of Oct.18, from Dr Plott, that he (had) received not any thing from you then, neither had seen the Catalogue (of Aubrey's manuscripts). Mr Ashmole is much vex't at my management of this businesse: but I must humbly beseech you to restrain your choler and passion for what I shall tell you. I told Mr Ashmole in May, before I came to Oxon, that You should have the Perusall of all, in the first place: I expected (you know) the receipt of the things while I was there (i.e. in Oxford): and he now tells me the reason is because that you are lookt upon as a Papist, and in these tumultuous Times your papers will be searcht (which is like enough, for people grow mad by charges of Papism), and so in leaving any thing in your hands, it would be a means to have them lost: wherefore (in passion) he desires that those papers that I conceive fitt to be kept secret, should be all sealed-up (after you have donne with them) and then putt in the Musaeum; not to be opened till after my death: and I thinke his advise is very solid and sedate. And you knowe, that in my Memoranda of Lives there are some things that may make me obnoxious to Scandalum Magnatum, and have heretofore written a letter or two which I wish were turnd to ashes.

New troubles arise upon me like Hydra's Heads; and my poore brother, whom I have injured, is very violent, and I must be faine shortly to take sanctuary again at Oxon ... When I was coming one time out of All-Soules, the Gapeabouts at the gate pointed at me and one said 'Romano-Catholicus'. I pray God bless and deliver you from such affronts. You know my Fate haz hindred me from study and reading much, so that I pretend but to little Learning, but for what I have donne by way of Excerpts, and preserving things from being lost, you know best of any one.

My heart is almost broke: and I have much adoe to keep up my poor spirits. I pray God comfort me. I hope between this and March to finish and digest my *Templa Druidum*, and if troubles come upon me, I will send all my MSS to you ...

All my bookes are now at Mr Hookes or Mr Kents; so that if I had leisure, I cannot enjoy them. Since my returne (from Oxford), I have been in Physic, or tumbling with porters etc. upon my removall: which is at present in an obscure place, to enjoy the society of an old acquaintance of mine ...

You see what falsity and ingratitude there is in the world. But if my brother should know of it, he would fall upon me like a Tygre. If that succeeds, I may be just to all my Creditors: and may be able to present a Honorary present to Mr Wood: and to print my Bookes etc. *Non est mortale quod opto* [What I wish for is not granted to mortals]. I desire of God almighty nothing but for the Publick good. Thus with my hearty prayers for you, I rest

Tuissimus, JA

> To divert my selfe since the Removall of my Bookes, I am perusing Ovid's Works, and I have halfe gonne it over, and have pickt up a sheet or more for my *Gentilisme*, even in his *Epistles* and *Amores*, where one would not expect it. You see what a strange distracted way of study the Fates give me ... I pray God blesse us both. (Tanner 456a, 34)

By 'my Gentilisme' Aubrey means *The Remaines of Gentilisme and Judaisme*, a collection of the rituals and superstitions of country people, some of which he shows to be descended from ancient pagan practices. He had begun to compile this collection in February 1687 and continued working on it until March 1689. It is the first book on English folklore and contains some fascinating accounts of practices which were not to survive much longer or were already obsolete. It is characteristic of Aubrey's extraordinary resilience that when he was beset by troubles on every side and reduced to a 'strange distracted way of study', he was still working on two original works. His frequent references to death at this time show that he felt with ever-increasing urgency that he must complete and arrange his writings in an intelligible form before it was too late.

'If my brother should know of it' – by 'it', Aubrey refers to the injury he has done William in his arrangements for the sale of Chalke; these included a reservation for himself (an annuity of £250), which he was keeping secret from William. At this stage Aubrey is clear that he has wronged his brother, but he has no intention of righting the wrong and is only afraid of what will happen if William learns of his scheme. And yet he refers to the 'falsity and ingratitude of the world', as though he were the injured party, a delusion which takes a stronger hold on him as time goes on, and he blames everything on William's imagined 'unkindness' and 'rough humour'. He tries to justify his dishonesty by saying that he hopes to be 'just to all my Creditors' and that 'I desire of God almighty nothing but for the Publick good'.

By chance eight letters from William dated between July 1688 and June 1690 survive amongst Aubrey's collection of letters from Virtuosi (A12, 176–84). From these there emerges a very different picture of the situation from that painted by Aubrey. When Aubrey deprived William of the management of the farm in 1683, he allowed him to continue to keep sheep on the downs and he supplemented his income by taking a job as Groom-Keeper of the Forest. When William of Orange came in, William, who was suspected of being a Catholic, lost his job as Groom-Keeper and the house that went with it. He wrote desperate letters to Aubrey, humbly asking for his help. Aubrey refused to meet him and kept him in the dark over his negotiations for the sale of Chalke. At first William is pathetically grateful for the help Aubrey is giving (whatever that may have been): 'I give you infinite thankes for your great care and trouble in my business' (21 May 1689); but by 17 June he knows that Aubrey is negotiating the sale of Chalke and is desperate: 'My humble and earnest request was, and still is, to speak with you ... and my principall desire is amity and love, and to acquit myself of those things which you shall be made sensible are falsely imputed to me.' Towards the end of this letter there is a note of reproach and hostility: 'I am not going to lawe unless forced ... If you will not consult me to prevent inconveniences that may insue, ruine will follow by this meanes ... and my poverty will be neither credit nor advantage to you.' In the last of these letters (13 June 1690) we find that William is a broken man, in poor health, in fear of imprisonment for debt, and still defending himself against Aubrey's charges of unkindness, while Aubrey still refuses to meet him.

Aubrey was a generous and humane man, much loved by a vast range of friends. It is hard to understand why he should have treated his brother so badly. It is almost as if he was in the grip of paranoia, convinced that William was the villain of the piece, persecuting him with unkindness and dishonesty.

By late December Wood, who was being thoroughly difficult, had still not delivered Aubrey's papers to Dr Plot, and Aubrey, for once, comes down hard on him:

Dec.22, 1688

Mr Wood,

Last Tuesday I went to see Mr Ashmole (whom I found ill). He lately received a letter from Dr Plott about the things I sent to Oxford and sayes that he desired you to send them to the Musaeum, but you denied it, and would not let him see the Catalogue that I sent. Mr Ashmole desired to speak with me about it, and was most outragiously angry, and charged me to write to you, as soon as I could, and to order you to putt the Box in the Musaeum: for he looks upon you as a P(apist) and sayeth so does the whole Universitie, and there was present at this angry fitt an Oxford scholar who owned what Mr Ashmole said. Mr Ashmole says that now there is such care and good method taken, that the Bookes in the Musaeum are more safe than those in the Library or Archives: and he expects to hear of your being plundered and papers burnt, as at the Spanish Ambassador's, at Wild House, where were burnt MSS and antiquities invaluable, such as are not left in the world, and he farther bids me tell you, that if you shall refuse to deliver the things sent downe by me to Oxford, that he will never look on you as a Friend and will never give a farthing more to the University of Oxford. I am very glad to hear by Dr Plott's letter to him the great care that is taken at the Musaeum to preserve the Bookes: and one, viz. the Keeper of the Musaeum, is to be present while the other party peruses the booke. Since therefore it is so order'd, I do desire and appoint you to send my Box forthwith (you may keep the key), for fear that all my MSS etc. should be rifled by the mobile (which God forbid but Mr E. Ashmole and I doe much fear it); besides my guift will make a better show in the Musaeum than when dispersed in 2 places.

When you see Mr Christopher White pray remember me to him. Let him give my laundresse, Mris Seacole, to keepe my shirts etc safe, for I was to have returned in a fortnight; but the Times prevented me.

I wish I could come to you in January or Feb. but somewhere I must retire about that time for fear of my brother and other Creditors. I wish you a merry Christmas,

Tuissimus, J.Albericus.

I have severall other MSS of my own and Mr Mercator's. That of mine that I most value is my Idea of the Education of a young Gentleman, which is a box as big as that I sent you; with choice Grammaticall bookes both ancient and moderne for the Informators [schoolmasters] to peruse and study. If I should die here, they would be lost or seized upon by Mr Kent's sonnes. If I send them to the Musaeum, the Tutors would burn it, for it crosses their interest exceedingly; if in your hands, when you die, your nephew will stop guns with them. I intended the Earl of Abingdon, but now he has other fish to fry. I think the Earl of Pembroke would do best, but had I the money to pay an amanuensis, I would leave a copy in the hands of each of these 2 peers.

I am mightily troubled and concerned for you, for feare of your writings being confounded by the mobile. Vivas et valeas. (A12, 1)

Since Aubrey's last letter to Wood, political events had moved fast. William had landed at Torbay on 5 November, and Abingdon had been amongst the first to join him in the West Country. William had entered London (18 December) and James fled from Rochester to France the very day Aubrey wrote this letter. There had been anti-Catholic riots in London: 'The rabble people demolish all Papists Chapells and severall popish Lords and Gent: houses, especialy that of the Spanish Ambassador, which they pillaged and burnt his Library etc.' (Evelyn Diary, 13 December 1688).

Christopher White was a chemist who lived in Holywell; he was Aubrey's landlord when he was staying in Oxford and sometimes provided him with cures.

Aubrey's fears for the papers he had left with Wood were rational, but his letter was hardly tactful; Wood must have been anxious enough already as he saw Catholics being arrested in Oxford, and the news that the whole university looked on him as a papist was hardly a comfort.

After a gap of six months in the surviving correspondence, Aubrey at last wrote to Wood, full of self-pity, but still working on *Monmenta Britannica*:

London, St Peters Day (= June 29), 1689

Mr Wood,

Oh the happy life that the innocent poore Hermits doe enjoy! You are not sensible of the Load of griefs and dayly vexation that some lie under. Notwithstanding which, considering that my candle burnes low, and that heart-breaking cares will shorten my life, I have forced my selfe from March 1st to transcribe: and one day with another I transcribe at least an hower. My Minutes were so confused and so interlined that (as you say) had I not donne it in my lifetime, they would have signified nothing. I have gone through the most difficult and perplext part, which by Michaelmass I shall end. But it is so: that a good part ought to be transcribed again: but now any one may understand it, and writing only on one side, the Minutes may be cutt and transposed. (F39, 386)

He wrote again to Wood in July, sending three full pages of answers to queries, and repeating that 'I have been (putting aside Law-businesse) wholly taken-up since the 1st March with transcribing, which in 6 weekes more I shall finish. If you etc had not importuned me to it, the collections would have been of no use; and then I shall come to you at Oxon and make my selfe happy in your good company' (F39, 389; 15 July 1689). He wrote once more in August when he claims to have almost finished transcribing, a gloomy letter, in which he seems to feel that death is imminent:

London, August 3, 1689

Deare Friend!

I sent you a letter dated July 23d: 'twas left at the shop with a young boy: I desire to know if you received it, so that in case it miscarried I may send you the same things while they are in my memory.

I have thanke God almost finish't my tedious Taske of transcribing. There are left 20 diatribes ... As soon as they are donne, I will send them to you for fear of Death's preventing me. For life is uncertain: and this morning I was anguished, and if I die before I send them to you, all will be lost, and there is no trust (hardly) in any body: and I know you are so much a Gentleman, that you will not doe me wrong by putting out another's Labours under your own name – a thing too common in this world.

About the middle of September I hope once more to be happy in your company at Oxon. Had you not goaded me on to putt my papers in order, I am satisfied they would have perished. I thanke you for it.

Vivas et valeas, tuissimus,
JA (F40, 372)

There is a sad irony in Aubrey's trust in Wood's integrity, for the wrong which he feared others would do him, was precisely what Wood was to do in *Athenae Oxonienses*, in which he ruthlessly used Aubrey's work without acknowledgement. Besides his other troubles Aubrey was beset by domestic difficulties at this time, which made work almost impossible:

London, Sept.5,1689

Mr Wood,

One would be apt to thinke (God blesse me) that there was an evil Genius did haunt me. I came to my pleasant Lodgeings at the end of January last, and a weeke after a school-master takes the chamber above me: comes-in at 12 or 1, and awakes me out of my sleep: and rises very early and falls a-hammering for a quarter of a hour or more, about his formes. The weeke after came a man and his wife and a child breeding teeth, that cries day and night, and the mother's shrill Tongue and singing to the cradle, in the next roome, is intolerable. But nothwithstanding this, I putt on a resolution to begin to transcribe on the 1st March. I had about a weekes work left, sc. to read over and correct and transcribe anew two Diatribes: when the child in the next chamber fell sick of the small-pox, and since, the mother: so that I was fayne to lye at Innes etc., because Mris Smyth is afrayd, never having had them and fatt: but I carried my MSS out with me: but want my Plinys and Homers etc. for quotations. I had the good luck lately to get a lodging in an empty house, where I have been layne 5 dayes, and am this day warn'd out for a new Tenant to come-in (I thought to have layne at Mr Kent's and he haz two children sick of the same disease.)

I intend by the middle of this month to come to Oxford and bring my MSS with me: and there finish them: which I could doe in a fortnight. In the mean time pray consider where I should lye: whether at Mr White's, and board there, or els at some other private place; I wish the window might be South or East. I left with my Laundresse, Mris Seacole by Mr White a shirt, cap, and cravat; for I intended to have returned in a fortnight but then the Prince of Orange came-in etc. I hope she haz not lost it; for I would not bring two shirts with me to stuff up my breeches and swelter me in the coach ...(Answers to Wood's queries) (F39, 395)

Through all this period of trouble and ill health Aubrey was attempting to transcribe and correct the *Monumenta Britannica*, to revise once more the *Natural History of Wilts*, and to continue his work on *Villare*, *Remaines of Gentilisme*, and the Lives of the English Mathematicians. He was still attending the meetings of the Royal Society, though not as regularly as in the past, and often spent the evenings with Hooke and other friends at coffee-houses. It was on the 15th of this month (September) that he spent the day with Hooke and composed a letter to Wood about the controversy with Newton.

Hooke had known Newton since the latter was elected a Fellow of the Royal Society in January 1672. Although Hooke, the acknowledged authority on light, had criticised some of Newton's theories and had incurred his rage, they had made it up and generally respected each other. But a far more bitter controversy was to arise when Newton published the first volume of his *Principia* in 1686. As Aubrey explains in the letter to Wood quoted below, Hooke had in 1670 given a lecture entitled 'An Attempt to prove the Motion of the Earth' which he later published. In this paper he had put forward three laws of planetary motion which were to be basic to Newton's *Principia*: 1. The law of universal gravity; 2. The law of inertia; 3. The supposition that the powers of gravity differ according to the distance between any two bodies. He wrote to Newton in 1679 when he published his theory and asked for his views on it and told him that he now calculated that the power of gravity decreases with the square of the distance. When Newton published the first volume of *Principia*, Hooke found that he had made no acknowledgement of what he had learnt from him. When Halley told him of Hooke's hurt at this, Newton went off the rails and wrote to Halley: 'He may do well in time to consider whether after this new provocation I be much bound (in doing him that justice which he claims) to make honourable mention of him in print, especially since this is the third time that he has given me trouble in this kind [the previous times were Hooke's criticisms of his theories of light]' (Newton Correspondence ii, 288; 20 June 1686). This quarrel was never made up and Hooke was deeply wounded.

In September 1689 Wood was writing an account of Hooke's life and Aubrey wrote to ask him to do Hooke justice; the letter is partly in Aubrey's hand, partly in Hooke's; Hooke takes over when matters become too complex for Aubrey:

September 15,1689

Mr Wood!

Mr Robert Hooke, R.S.S., did in anno 1670, write a discourse, called, *'An Attempt to prove the motion of the Earth,'* which he then read to the Royal Society; but printed it in the beginning of the year 1674, wherein he haz delivered the theorie of explaining the coelestial motions mechanically; his words are these, viz.:

'I shall only for the present hint that I have in some of my foregoing observations discovered some new motions even in the Earth itself, which perhaps were not dreamt of before, which I shall hereafter more at large describe, when further tryalls have more fully confirmed and compleated these beginnings. At which time also I shall explaine a systeme of the world, differing in many particulars from any yet known, answering in all things to the common rules of mechanicall motions. This depends upon 3 suppositions; first, that all coelestiall bodys whatsoever have an attractive or gravitating power towards their own centers, whereby they attract not only their own parts, and keep them from flying from them, as we may observe the Earth to doe, but that they doe also attract all the other coelestiall bodys that are within the sphere of their activity, and consequently that not only the Sun and Moon have an influence upon the body and motion of the Earth, and the Earth upon them, but that Mercury also, Venus, Mars, Saturne, and Jupiter, by their attractive powers have a considerable influence upon its motion, as, in the same manner, the corresponding attractive power of Earth hath a considerable influence upon their motions also. The second supposition is this, that all bodys whatsoever, that are putt into direct and simple motion will soe continue to move forwards in a straight line, till they are by some other effectuall powers deflected and bent into a motion describing a circle, ellipsis, or some other uncompounded curve line. The third supposition is, that these attractive powers are so much the more powerfull in operating, by how much nearer the body wrought upon is to their own centers. Now what these severall degrees are, I have not yet experimentally verified ... But it is a notion which if fully prosecuted, as it ought to be, will mightily assist the astronomers to reduce all the coelestiall motions to a certaine rule, which I doubt will never be done true without it ...'

About 9 or 10 years ago, Mr Hooke writt to Mr Isaac Newton of Trinity College, Cambridge, to make a demonstration of this theory, not telling him, at first, the proportion of the gravity to the distance, nor what was the curv'd line that was thereby made. Mr Newton, in his answer to the letter, did expresse that he had not knowne of it; and in his first attempt about it, he calculated the curve by supposing the attraction to be the same at all distances: upon which, Mr Hooke sent, in his next letter, the whole of his hypothesis, scilicet, that the gravitation was reciprocall to the square of the distance, ... concerning which Mr Newton hath a demonstration, not at all owning he receiv'd the first intimation of it from Mr Hooke. Likewise Mr Newton haz in the same booke printed some other theories and experiments of Mr Hooke, as about the oval figure of the Earth and sea, without acknowledgement from whom he had them.

Mr Wood! This is the greatest discovery in nature that ever was since the world's creation. It never was so much as hinted by any man before. I know you will doe him right. I hope you may read his hand. I wish he had writt plainer, and afforded a little more paper.

Tuus,
J.Aubrey

> Before I leave this towne, I will gett of him a catalogue of what he hath wrote; and as much of his inventions as I can. But they are many hundreds; he believes not fewer than a thousand. 'Tis such a hard matter to get people to doe themselves right. (B.L. Hooke 412–5)

It looks as if Aubrey had now obstinately closed his eyes to mundane and law business, including William's distress, and concentrated on what he considered more important – the intellectual world – desperately trying to get his papers in order before death struck.

Chapter XIV

'I have undonne my Brother and my selfe' 1689–93

THE FIRST VOLUME OF *Athenae Oxonienses* was now in the press and Wood intensified the demands he made on Aubrey, making no allowance for the difficulties under which he worked. His letters became increasingly peremptory and discourteous; at the end of November he wrote:

St Andrews Day, 89

Mr Aubrey,

You told me in your last you had a good deal of stuff from Mr Henshaw concerning Nick Hill ... and none of these things, or of your self, have I heard or seen. You told me also you would send to Olor Iscanus [Henry Vaughan] about my Queries ... as without doubt you have done, but why doth he not answer you?

Why have you not spoke to Mr Ashmole to let me have some minutes concerning the life of Will. Lilly – and why do you not send me word whether Mr John Rushworth be living or dead?

Aubrey never showed the slightest resentment at the way Wood treated him. A later letter shows that he had in fact written to Vaughan four times but had no reply, and that Ashmole was too old and sick to deal with any queries. Rushworth was an historian who had died in the debtors' prison, as Aubrey tells him in a letter of the following July.

When Aubrey next wrote to Wood, the following January, he was expecting to be engaged in a Chancery Suit which he had previously waved; this must have been concerned with the legal problems involved in selling the lease of Broad Chalke and William's rights:

London, Jan.16, 1690

Mr Wood,

I delivered yesterday at the Warehouse at the Saracen's Head a bundle of papers for you ...

You may thinke it strange that I have been so long silent; but for that I shall give you an account next weeke. I have been extremely busy; and I much fear next Terme I shall be engaged in more trouble. I waved a

Chancery Suite two terms when I was at Oxford, which was the reason I stayed there so long ...

I have now putt in pretty good order, understandably, my *Monumenta Britannica*, which is about 7 quires ...

Tuissimus, JA

The child in the next Chamber to me is of late much quieter, so that last month I writt faire and corrected the Preface. (A12, 11)

The Preface to the Monumenta Britannica (see Appendix III) is one of Aubrey's finest pieces, completed under appalling conditions.

In April he wrote a long and discursive letter, apologising for 'my half years silence' (he evidently forgot that he had in fact written in January). This letter is shot through with gloom, and ends with the assertion that after one more short visit to complete business he will never visit Oxford again; even Oxford has betrayed him, 'for it seems I am a derision to them'. He was clearly in a deep depression:

London, April 24,1690

Mr Wood!

I doe beg your pardon for my half years silence, and I shall now send you an account of my Life from Michaelmas last to this time. By the beginning of October last I had made an end of my *Monumenta Britannica*, 3 volumes, and one other vol. of Miscellanea, all which I shall send you, God willing, next weeke.

After Michaelmass I parted with Chalke Farme to Mr Kent, to my great griefe, which I putt-off as well as I can, and I cannot doe it better then by putting my papers in some method before I dye; for I have a good deale of worke upon the loome. About the middle of October ... Mr Kent and all his family went to Chalke; ... And there we were to goe to settle matters, and I thought to have sent some good old Bookes to Oxon; but my brother, in whose custody they were, would not be spoken to and absented himselfe. At Christmas I thought to have gonne thither with Mr K. but did not, and then my brother and he mett; and I am afraid between my brother and Mr Kents sonne (a Westminster scholar) all my best things are imbezilled. God help the helpless. Mr K. is there now but I shortly expect his returne and then I shall tell you when I shall come to Oxon, which I doe intend at farthest about Whitsuntide.

For these 3 last moneths I have followed close my Naturall History, and have been ill 2 months of the time with the stone and Gowte, but not very severe (except the stone 2 dayes).

[Over 2 pages of answers to Wood's queries]

In March last it cost me 3 dayes paines to make a collection of all my learned and Philosophicall Letters, which now make a faire Volume, viz. from 1643 to this yeare [= A12 and 13]. You may pick something out of them. 'Tis pity they should be putt under pies, as the Bishop of Sarums were ...

Pray consider where I should lye when I come to you: for I shall stay but a little while and have but little money to spare: and a good deale of businesse to doe there: and I never intend to see the place again, for it seems I am a derision to 'em: and I will wash my hands of them and the place. (F39, 402)

Attached to this letter is another, written on the back of a letter to Aubrey, which appears to be a continuation (it has no date or place); it shows how the question of safeguarding his manuscripts still weighs heavily on his mind:

I am sorry my paper is so bad: I pray God you may read this letter ...

Mr Wood, I know you love me, and take you to be my faithfull friend: I am in a Dilemma and know not well what to doe as to securing my MSS. Mr Ashmole etc. advise me by all meanes to secure them in the Musaeum; which (I grant) would be safe; but many parts want a little transcribing; and if I dye before they are printed, my Will and intention and desire is that you might have the Benefit of them as well as care. But if they are deposited in the Musaeum, Dr Plott or etc. will and must have the benefit; and (no doubt) would have the credit too; which I verily believe you would not doe. You are not very young, and a mortall man, and when you dye, your Nephew stoppes gunnes with them, or are putt under pies. What should I doe in this Case? When I come to Oxon, I will make a short Will as to these MSS to give you title to them.

To make you merry, I'le tell you a story that Dr Henry Birket told us tother day at his cousen [Thomas] Mariet's, sc. that about 1638 or 1640 when he was of Trinity College, Dr Kettle, preaching as he was wont to doe on Trinity Sunday, told 'em that they should keepe their bodies chast and holy: 'but,' said he, 'you Fellows of the College here eate good commons and drinke good double-beer, and breede seede, and that will gett-out.' How would the good old Doctor have raunted and beat-up his kettle-drum, if he should have seen such luxury in the College as there is now! *Tempora mutantur* [Times change].

I have taken care with the deliverer of the Post letters to secure them for me. For Mr Hook is not, or will not, be within almost all day long. He lies abed all the morning, sitting up at study all night: and the afternoons he goes about business: so that the post-men were weary with being so often disappointed ... (F39, 400)

A feature of this letter is Aubrey's suspicion that all, except Wood, are against him; Plot will take credit for his writings, Wood's nephew would stop guns with them; William and Kent's son have embezzled his best things (in fact William's letters show that he went to a good deal of trouble to save Aubrey's books and papers, refusing to give Kent the key to Aubrey's study); worst of all, Oxford has turned against him and he is 'a derision to them'. What makes him say this we do not know, but he wrote to Wood that one of the Fellows had said that his Villare Anglicanum was a 'whimwham'.

Even in the encircling gloom, when his thoughts dwell continually on the prospect of death, he can rouse himself to tell an excellent anecdote 'to make you merry', but his next letter shows him still deeply depressed:

London, May 10th, 1690

Mr Wood,

I sent you a long letter in folio 5 sides ... I hope you are still in the land of the Living; pray faile not to write by the next post. So let me know if you received my letter. If not I must endeavour to enquire for it: I shall never remember all the Contents again. Upon the receipt of yours I will by the next waggon send down a box full of MSS and printed bookes ... In my next I shall send you three or four obits ... I wish heartily my papers were in your hands, for Death seemes to threaten. God blesse you and me in this in-and-out world. (Ballard 14, 142)

When Aubrey next writes to Wood (July), enclosing answers to yet another set of queries, he gives a picture of William's behaviour which is quite inconsistent with what we learn from William's own letters:

London, July 5, 1690

Mr Wood,

I have now with much difficulty answered these Queries, for I am faine to lye dormant for feare of an Arrest, which will come to a matter of 90li, which my Brother might have compounded for 12. His rough humour hath putt all my business so out of order that it hath also made me doe him great prejudice, and I have had to doe with some odd people.

Heu, heu, quid faciant homines, cuive habeant fidem? [Alas, alas! what are men to do or in whom should they put their trust? Catullus 30, 6] I hope to get a Protection in a short time. The Royal Society have donne me the honour to be at the charge of a Transcript of my Naturall Historie, which is deposited in Mr Hooke's hands. John Rushworth of Lincone's-Inne Esq (historian) died in the Rules-court in Southwarke at the widow Bayley's house (a good woman and who was very careful and tendfull of him) ... If I am caught by the Bayliffs (my brother having been so unkind), I will end my daies with that good woman Mris Baylie. But I most extremely desire first to see Oxon once more to put my writings in order, and then I am ready for death or arrest. I hope to come to you after the Act is over.

Mr Kent's mayd is a giddy wench, and puttes my letters in her boxe of worke, that 'tis like looking for a needle in a bottle of hay, and one letter she lost out of her breast ...

The transcript of Aubrey's *Natural History of Wiltshire* is still in the Royal Society Library (MS 92); he says in a later letter to Wood (F29, 429; 2 August 1691): 'the transcribing of both parts hath cost the R.S. £7 with the paper. 'Tis a folio as thick as the Common Prayer Booke. I did not think it would have proved so bulky.' It was indeed a great honour that the Society had gone to this expense, since they were always short of money.

Although he says he hopes to get a protection soon, Aubrey is resigned to the prospect of ending his days in the debtors' prison (Rules-court Alley), where the historian John Rushworth had died the previous May. He blames William's unkindness for his predicament but admits again that he has done his brother 'great prejudice'.

He added a P.S. to this letter:

July 10

> Since my former part of the letter, I met Dr Plot, who told me he would carry downe and see safe the things that I should send to the Musaeum, and to you. Accordingly on Munday last, I brought him 2 boxes and a great bundle of bookes. In the Box I have this day sent downe to you by the Saracens Head Carrier (carriage payd) I had putt 4 volumes of MSS of my owne in folio besides a thick Folio of Letters to me. But yesterday the Royal Society hearing of it were all up-on-end, and would not have a denyall, but that I must stay the MSS and they will be at the charge of transcribing them. I could not disobey their order, and did not expect so great an honour from them ... I would willingly print my Templa Druidum in my life time; for that is finished; only wants an Aristarchus to polish the style ... Pray let me heare from you by the next post. Vale. Without faile, for my satisfaction that the things are come safe to Oxon: for I heare there is exceeding robbing. (F39, 405)

Wood continued to flood Aubrey with queries, quite regardless of his troubles; he sends a list at the end of December saying, 'You know my book is in the press and therefore delay not' (F45, 204; 27 December 1690). And Aubrey faithfully continued to send him answers. But when he wrote on 4 January, he was more concerned with William's imagined unkindnesses, in a letter which is a tissue of self-deception, hypocrisy and dishonesty:

Jan.4th,1691

> Deare Friend!
>
> I shall send to you next weeke (to be deposited at the Musaeum until further order) 2 excellent Tomes of Ven. Bede; they are not designed for the Museum, nor Bodl.Libr. Pray ask if there is or like to be any Library at New Inne. If so, I would give it there: if not Jesus Coll. Library.

> I am mightily discomposed about my brother; I intrusted him with my estate at Chalke (250li per annum) almost two yeares. I desired him to pay Captain Stumpe of Malmesbury a debt of 20li upon Bond, borrowed in 1660, and he was so civill as to accept the principall. And my brother never did it: also to take up a debt of 80li besides interest, which was offered to him for 12li. And he never did it: and I never received from him for all that time from that estate but 12li 6d, which disgusted me so much that I threw my selfe upon Mr Kent and he shall appease my Creditors; and besides I shall be in danger of imprisonment. But nothing does wound me so much as my poor Creditors. Had my brother been but ordinarily civill to me, I could have confirmed the estate upon him. Now, how can you thinke but I must be continually troubled in mind? I have not been able to write since I sawe you, but I hope to pluck up my spirits the next week and I doe but desire to finish the second part of my Naturall History of Wilts. But I am afraid I must goe downe into Wilts before the end of this month, and that will putt these designes out of order ...
>
> I suspect my brother (knowing the intimacy between you and me) may ask a trepanning [= entrapping] question whether I have an Annuity from Mr Kent for Chalke. If he should know of it, he would seize upon it. I expect the next terme to be engaged in a Suite in Chancery of which I shall never live to see the end. God blesse me and helpe all helpeless and shiftlesse people. (F39, 411)

This is a very confused letter; events spread over many years are intermingled in a mind which has long been brooding over imagined wrongs. He 'intrusted' Chalk to William soon after Tom's death in 1681 and took it away from him in 1683, when there was a terrible quarrel between them (see page 110). But negotiations with Kent did not begin until after his mother's death in 1686. It seems that part of the bargain with Kent was that besides paying an annuity of £250, he should pay off Aubrey's debts. As for Aubrey's 'poor creditors', he nowhere else shows any sympathy for them; his only concern was to escape the bailiffs. We see in this letter the first explicit reference to the annuity he is to receive from Kent and confirmation that he is hiding this from William. Little wonder that he is 'continually troubled in mind'.

(Captain Stump: in Part 2 of the Natural History of Wilts (Chapter 1) Aubrey has a 'digression', a story too good to omit: Captain Thomas Stump of Malmesbury. 'Tis pity the strange adventures of him should be forgotten. He was the eldest son of Mr Will. Stump, rector of Yatton Keynell; was a boy of the most daring spirit; he would climb towers and trees most dangerously; nay, he would walk on the battlements there. He had too much spirit to be a scholar, and about 16 went on a voyage with his uncle, since Sr Thomas Ivy, to Guyana in anno 1633, or 1632. When the ship putt in somewhere there, four or five of them straggled into the country too far, and in the interim the wind served, and the sailes were hoist, and the stragglers left behind. It was not long before the wild people seized on them and strip't them, and those that had beards they knocked their braines out and (as I remember) did eat them; but the Queen saved T. Stump and the other boy. Stump threw himself into the river Oronoque to have drowned himself but could not sinke; he is very full-chested. The other youth died shortly. He lived among them till 1636 or 1637. His narrations are very strange and pleasant; but so many years since have made me almost forget all. He sayes there is incomparable fruite there, and that it may be termed the paradise of the world. He says that the spondyles of the backbones of the huge serpents there are used to sitt on, as our women sit upon butts. He taught them to build hovills, and to thatch and wattle. I wish I had a good account of his abode there; he is *fide dignus* [a reliable witness]. I never heard of any man who lived so long among those savages. A ship then sayling by, a Portughese, he swam to it; and they took him up and made use of him for a sea-boy. As he was sayling near Cornwall he stole out of a port-hole and swam to shore; and so begged to his father's in Wiltshire. When he came home, nobody knew him, and they would not own him: only Jo. Harris the carpenter knew him. At last he recounted so many circumstances that he was owned, and in 1642 had a commission for a Captain of Foot in King Charles the First's army.')

In a letter of 4 February (1691) including yet more answers to queries, Aubrey says:

> I have now donne my Naturall Historie of Wilts within three chapters. So that I am now contented to resigne up my animula [soul], when it shall please God to call for it ... At the latter end of the Terme I expect my brother to come like a Fury, to fall upon me and Mr Kent: and very likely I may be arrested. (F39, 414)

During the next six months Aubrey wrote frequently answering Wood's continuous stream of queries, but there is no more mention of legal troubles; the lease to Kent, dated 21 April 1691 in the Wilton Survey Book, seems to have settled the matter for the time being. He planned to visit Oxford in September but found the coach full:

> I gave earnest to come to Oxon on friday last: but when I was to goe to the coach I found 5 woemen: and two of them old and very sick: and no roome for my Bitch. So I have deferred it till Munday but it would be hard if I should lose my Earnest ... on Munday night (God willing) I shall be at Oxford. I shall come weary. Pray consider where I shall lodge: for I shall stay but for a weeke, and perhaps Mr White would not foul his sheetes for so little time. I ought to be pretty neer to you.

We hear more about his bitch the following year: 'My pretty little bitch is with puppy and I am much concerned to leave her behind me; she was lined by a most curious little Spaniel. I could afford to bring her with me [to Oxford] (Tanner 456a, 40; 19 May, 1692).

After he had returned from his visit, he wrote to Wood:

London, October 27,1691

Deare Friend,

In the first place I returne you my hearty Thankes for your Civilities to me and for my good Entertainment at Oxford, and for your kind Token. I thanke God I have yet my Liberty: Mr Kent compounded the debt that I was arrested for: but I dread the end of this Terme. My brother haz been unkind to me and (God forgive me) I have undonne him and my selfe. Hereafter, when your businesse is over [i.e. *Athenae Oxonienses Vol.2* published], I will give you a state of that matter: but the trueth is, I was never made to manage an estate and was predestinated to be cosen'd and cheated. (F39, 435)

Here we have Aubrey's frankest admission that he has 'undonne' William. The sale of the lease of Broad Chalke to Matthew Kent left William with no source of income. But how had Aubrey undone himself? How had he been 'cosen'd and cheated'? Aubrey seems to have made a thoroughly good bargain with Kent. We have hints later that he was on good terms with him, who forwarded to the Ashmolean at Aubrey's request presents of books from his library still lying at Chalke. Moreover, we hear no more of creditors and dangers of arrest in the remaining correspondence.

But William continued to dispute the legal validity of the sale. By March (1692) a threatened suit in Chancery loomed uncomfortably near:

Yesterday my brother came to Towne and this day is gonne into Sussex, and I am served with a Subpoena, as also Mr Kent. So that I have got a newe suite that I never expect to weare out. God help the oppressed. (Ballard 14, 146)

It was not until October of the following year that William's case against Kent came to court; Aubrey wrote to Wood, while staying with Lord Abingdon at Lavington, expecting to be summoned to give evidence and determined at the last to 'doe him right, though to my owne hindrance':

I have retirement and leisure enough, and have read over Mr Locke's book [John Locke, *On Education*, 1693]: but when I come to London I shall be ready to sinke under the trouble I am comeing into: viz. Mr Kent and my brother are up to their eares in Chancery, and I shall be drawne

> in: though my brother hath not been so kind to me as he ought to have been, which has happened exceedingly to his prejudice, for he might have had Chalke Farm, now let for 250li per annum, yet when I come upon oath, I must doe him right, though to my owne hinderance. (F51, 6, 21 October 1693)

Aubrey seems to have done well out of the arrangements, for we hear no more of his being pursued by creditors; Kent evidently kept his side of the bargain, paying Aubrey's debts besides the annuity of £250, which would have been sufficient for his needs. Later we find William living with Mr Stokes again at Kington Manor and no longer, apparently, destitute. Perhaps Aubrey may have eventually paid William a proportion of the annuity. Relations between the brothers seem to have improved; in 1693 William was working with the young Tanner in an attempt to complete Aubrey's Antiquities of Wiltshire (see Chapter XI), and Aubrey wrote to Tanner: 'I take your Civility to my Brother as donne to my selfe; and I hope you and he may live to finish *Wiltshire Antiquities*.' There is one further mention of the dispute over Chalke in Aubrey's surviving correspondence; William Holder writing to him on 2 July 1695 wishes him 'a happy end of your lawsuit' (A12, 173). So the case evidently lingered on. We do not know when it ended; after Aubrey's death, William, in a letter to Tanner of 27 October 1699, says: 'I am still in hopes to get possession of Chalke Farm', which can only mean that he intended to persevere in the lawsuit. But it was an idle hope; a new lease of the previous March had finally severed all connections with the Aubreys, and William lived out his days at Kington, dying, in debt, in 1703.

Chapter XV

Monumenta Britannica *and* Athenae Oxonienses *1691–93*

WOOD, WITH HIS BOOK NOW IN THE PRESS, continued to flood Aubrey with queries: 'you must without delay get the Christian name of ...'; 'The next thing I would have you do ...'; 'Tell me also ...' (F45, 176; 22 January 1692)

In January 1691 Aubrey wrote to Wood to try to get him to revise his account of Hooke:

London Jan.20.1691

Mr Wood,

Whatever you doe, pray take a special care to doe Mr Hooke right against Mr Isaac Newton; it is the greatest discovery ever yet was made, and Mr Newton runnes away with the glory of it. When I sent you my box last, I enclosed in it an exact account of Mr Hooke's case, writt with his owne hand: I perceiv'd you had not taken notice of it. (F39, 412)

But Wood disliked Hooke and never 'did him right', although he wrote to Aubrey that he would do so, as we learn from a letter of Aubrey: 'Mr Hooke haz been very ill; we were afraid we should have lost him; he was glad to be assured from me that you would doe him Right against Mr Newton; it comforted his spirits ...' (F39, 424; 21 April 1691)

By now Aubrey had made new friends in Oxford, above all Edward Llwyd (1660-1709). He had been Plot's assistant at the Ashmolean Museum and took over as Keeper in 1691; he was distinguished as a naturalist, a Celtic scholar and a philologist.

Aubrey was already planning to transfer his papers from Wood's custody to the Ashmolean and was starting to donate manuscripts, books and antiquities to the Museum. He quickly established a happy relationship with Llwyd, who came to replace Wood as Aubrey's principal correspondent in Oxford (thirty letters survive from Aubrey to Llwyd, and thirteen from Llwyd to Aubrey). The first surviving letter from Llwyd shows that he had a great respect for Aubrey and was eager to help him:

The Old Ashmolean, engraved by Michael Burghers, 1685; by kind permisssion of the Curator of the museum of the History of Science, Oxford

Oxford Febr.12,1691

Honoured Sir,

I received your obliging letter, and also the present you have been pleased to send us; I have disposed of the hands [= handiworks, works of art?] according to your directions, and doe assure you that as I am sensible of your continual favours to our Museum, and of the respects due to you from all men that value learning and have the happinesse of knowing you; soe you shoulde allways find me very ready and forward to doe you any small service that lies in my power. I remember when we talk'd last together at Mr Wyldes, you were pleas'd to tell me you had some Queries to propose to me wherein perchance I might be able to give some satisfaction in regard I understood Welsh. If you have any such questions at present and are disposed to take the trouble of sending them to me, you will soon receive such answers as may be given by,

Sir, Your very humble Servant,
Edw. Llywd. (A12, 240)

Aubrey for his part recognised Llwyd's ability; in a P.S. to a letter answering Wood's queries, he says: 'When I have convenience, I will send to Mr Llwyd my *Villare*: no man can doe the British part better, which is the thing I chiefly aim at' (F39, 148; 17 February 1691). In April he duly got Wood to deliver the manuscript of the *Villare* to Llwyd, together with a letter in which he asks him to complete it, which he enthusisatically agreed to do, being qualified by his knowledge of Welsh and Gaelic.

Aubrey was now making serious efforts to get *Monumenta Britannica* printed but had difficulty in finding a publisher who would undertake it. Although he had tried to get the manuscript in order in the summer of 1689, a great deal of it was still chaotic; in a letter to Wood of 29 June 1689 he had said:

> My Minutes were so confused and so interlined that (as you say) had I not donne it in my lifetime they would have signified nothing. I have gonne through the most difficult and perplext part, which by Michaelmas I shall end. But it is so, that a good part ought to be transcribed again: but now anyone may understand it, and writing only on one side, the Minutes may be cutt and transposed. (F39, 386)

He continued to work on it, adding new material as well as transcribing the old, but he never got it into a fit state for publication. In May 1692 a bookseller and stationer called Christopher Wilkinson showed interest, but he must have changed his mind on seeing the manuscript.

In February 1693 Aubrey wrote to Llwyd that he had decided to print it by subscription:

> London, Feb 4, 1693
>
> Worthy Friend,
>
> I have received your obligeing letter but multiplicity of businesse hindred me from writing to you ... I thought to have dealt with some Bookeseller to print my Book. I have tryed severall, and though they are satisfyed the Booke will sell well, paper being so deare, they will not venture above a booke of 5s price.
>
> My three, or rather 4, volumes (for I will add my Miscellanea) will not be lesse than 15s; from Mr Smyth of Paule church yard: who (as all others) advise me to gett Subscriptions and to print it at Oxford. So on Monday next I will put Subscriptions into the Press, and will send 100 or 200 to Oxford, where I shall want your assistance. (Ashmole 1814, 102)

He wrote the same month to Edmund Gibson for advice and help. Gibson was a brilliant young fellow of Queen's College, an antiquarian. He had just published an edition of the *Saxon Chronicle* (1692) and was now in charge of making a revision of Camden's *Britannia* with the assistance of Llwyd. Gibson replied with a letter which was sympathetic but not altogether helpful; he was perhaps embarrassed by the fact that proposals for the printing of his revision of Camden were about to come out.

The following month Thomas Tanner wrote offering his help; he was another Wiltshire man (his father was Vicar of Market Lavington), still an undergraduate at the Queen's College; a keen and talented antiquarian, he had been enrolled by Gibson to contribute to the revision of Camden by supplying information on his native county:

> Queen's Coll., March 7, 1693
>
> Worthy Sir,
>
> The welcome news you were pleased to send us not long since in your letter to Mr Gibson (concerning the fair progress you have made towards the printing of your *Monumenta Britannica*) hath caused me to give you the trouble of these lines ... I hope Mr Gibsons reasons against printing your book at Oxon will not be so prevalent ... as to hinder us of your good company, which upon that account we should so long here enjoy. (A13, 198)

Aubrey continued to try to get *Monumenta Britannica* published until the year of his death; it was undoubtedly his most important work. The Prefaces, both to Part 1 *Templa Druidum* (see Appendix III), and Part 2, Camps etc. are masterly and the body of the work contains much archaeological evidence which would otherwise have been lost and set new standards in archaeological survey; Stuart Pigott says: 'The objective field surveys of Aubrey and Stukely at Stonehenge and Avebury are today more valuable than nearly the whole huge output of nineteenth century literature on the same monuments' (*William Stukely*, p. 18). But more importantly it shows a new attitude to historical study, relying on material remains to reconstruct the past instead of written records. It is 'the first English book that can be called "archaeological" in the modern sense' (Hunter, p. 159). His careful records, made on the spot, and his comparative method produced some important new discoveries, in particular the dating of the megalithic monuments. Moreover, the work was an inspiration to later antiquarians, such as Stukeley, who made lengthy notes from Gale's copy. His contemporaries, including Dugdale, the greatest antiquarian of the time, and John Locke the philosopher, who was prepared to print it at his own expense, recognised the novelty and value of Aubrey's work. But it was never ready for the press and no publisher could ever have undertaken it.

When Gibson saw the manuscript, he wrote to Tanner: 'The accounts of things are soe broken and short, the parts so much disordered, and the whole such a mere Rhapsody, that I cannot but wonder how that poor man could entertain any thoughts of a present impression. They will be serviceable enough, however, especially in Counties where Intelligence falls short; but in the rest, we shall not make much use of them' (Gibson-Tanner, Tanner 25, 134; 12 April 1694). In the revision of Camden, *Monumenta Britannica* is quoted five or six times with acknowledgement and through this Aubrey's name as an antiquary survived.

On 18 June 1691 the first volume of Wood's *Athenae et Fasti Oxonienses* was published in London, being 'An exact History of all the Writers and Bishops who have had their Education in the most Antient and Famous University of Oxford from the fifteenth year of King Henry the Seventh, 1500 to 1690, to which are added the Fasti or Annales of the said University'. It is a massive work of painstaking scholarship, comprising 874 lives in Volume 1, and 611 in Volume 2, published the following year, some only a few lines long, but very many of considerable extent. In addition to these, Wood was preparing a third volume; 500 more lives were added to the second edition (1723), all taken from the notes he had made.

Wood treats his subject chronologically, the first volume reaching only to 1640. Within a week of publication Dr Charlett, Master of University College, told Wood he had received a letter saying that 'a great deal of ill nature was expressed in my book lately published'; Wood exclaims indignantly: 'Who is ill natur'd? Whether the author who speaks the truth, or a company of idle fellows that sit all day in an alehouse or tavern to pick holes in the coates of industrious men who labour for the honour of the University?' (L & T iii, 365). And soon there was the inevitable charge that there was a 'great deal of popery' in it.

Bathurst criticised its style: 'Mr Charlet told me that the President of Trinity College said that "I *collected* it but not *writ* it", that is in good language.' There is truth in this criticism; the style is plain and unadorned, a compilation rather than a work of literature; in fact it is almost true to say that it only achieves literary grace when instead of paraphrasing Aubrey's notes, Wood actually quotes him verbatim. These quotations shine out like a beacon in the midst of the drabness of Wood's own narrative.

Wood nowhere acknowledges the help he had received from Aubrey and in the whole work mentions him only twice, once as a member of Harrington's Rota Club, once in connection with Blackburne's Life of Hobbes, 'the materials of which were all, or at least for the most part, taken from the English life of Thomas Hobbes, largely and more punctually written by John Aubrey, his antient acquaintance ...'

(Ath.Ox.2, 647). Wood's debt to Aubrey was immense, and his treatment of him disgraceful; he did not even give him a copy of the book.

If the reception of the first volume was hostile, it was nothing to the storm which was to break when on 18 July of the following year (1692) the second volume was published in London. The day after its arrival in Oxford, Wood met Dr Charlett, Master of University College, who told him that 'Dr John Wallis was angry and would complaine and have satisfaction for what is said of him in my second volume' (L & T III, 395). Mr Harris of Jesus College 'told me that I had set all Oxford in a flame'. 'All people endeavour to pick out such things that are bad from it, and mention nothing good, and say I abuse all people and speak well of none.'

Wood wrote asking Aubrey how his book had been received in London. Aubrey had been staying in Essex with John Ray, the father of English botany and zoology, a close friend and percipient critic of Aubrey's works. After returning to London, Aubrey replied in a letter which scarcely disguised the hurt he had suffered from Wood's treatment of him:

London, Aug. 20, 1692

Mr Wood,

I am returned from Essex and have received your two letters and Dr Gale hath received your two volumes. I shall not be able to tell you what censure is passed upon them till October next. The Royal Society is adjourned till the 18th October.

But accidentally I spoke to Mr Gadbury, who is extremely incenst against you: he tells me what you have wrote, and I am sorry for it. For he was civil to you and is an ingeniose Loyall person; and he sayes you have printed lyes concerning him: and he wonders you should meddle with him having never been of the University ...

I saw your bookes at Dr Gales and turnd them over: you have not inserted some Epitaphs which I sent you. (F51, 4)

It is clear from the last sentence that Wood had not even sent Aubrey copies of his book. Thomas Gale (1635–1702) was at this time High Master of St Paul's; he was a fellow of the Royal Society and a close friend of Aubrey, who often stayed with him. He was one of the leading scholars of the period who wrote many works on history and literature; he admired Aubrey's *Monumenta Britannica* of which he made an annotated copy. Gadbury was the leading astrologer of the time. He had not been educated at Oxford and so there was no reason why Wood should have mentioned him at all, but he tacked onto the life of another astrologer, Sir George Wharton, a brief sketch of his career which is malicious; it dwells on Gadbury's humble origins, shows that he had not, as most supposed, been educated at Oxford, and refers disparagingly to his achievements in astrology as fortune-telling. Gadbury was naturally furious, and Wood's specious reply to Aubrey was not calculated to cool his anger:

> I wonder at nothing more than that Mr Gadbury should take it amiss of those things that I say of him, for whereas the generality of scholars did formerly take him to have been bred an Academician because he was born at Oxon and consequently not to be much admired, now their eyes being opened and knowing that his education hath been mechanicall they esteem him a prodigy of parts and therefore are much desirous that his picture may hang in the public Gallery at the Schooles. Pray remember me to him and desire him that if I speake any things that are untrue, he may rectifie them: put them into your hands and to be sent to me. (A.W. to J.A., Ballard 14, 154; no date)

If Wood could afford to incur the hostility of Gadbury to satisfy his malicious streak, this self-indulgence was to bring him serious trouble in another case. Aubrey had repeatedly warned Wood not to let his Lives get abroad, because of the risk of offending powerful men, for instance: 'I do earnestly desire you not to lett my MSS of Lives to goe out of your hands; for there is a *Scandalum Magnatum* (Scandal against Great Men)' (F39, 360). But Wood did not apply this lesson to himself in writing the life of Judge David Jenkins of Glamorganshire. Jenkins had been a stalwart royalist during the Civil War and one of the judges for South Wales. Aubrey had originally supplied Wood with an account of him in a letter of 16 January 1672 (F39, 160) (see page 36) and gave an almost identical account in *Brief Lives*, ending:

> Tis pity he was not made one of the judges of Westminster-hall for his long sufferings; and he might have been, he told me, if he had given money to the Chancellor – but he scorned it' (B.L. David Jenkins)

Wood followed Aubrey closely in his life of Jenkins (II, 219), including the sentence: 'After the Restauration of King Charles II 'twas expected by all that he should be made one of the Judges in Westminster Hall, and so he might have been, would he have given money to the then Lord Chancellor.'

The Lord Chancellor concerned was the great Edward Hyde, Earl of Clarendon, the minister on whom Charles II most relied until he was impeached by a hostile Commons and banished in 1667/8. The seventeen charges brought against him included the sale of offices, but he said of himself: 'His integrity was ever without blemish, and believed to be above temptation.' Wood should have known that his son Henry was unlikely to let such a slight on his father's honour pass unpunished.

Henry complained to the university authorities that his father had been libelled, and a prosecution for *Scandalum Magnatum* was initiated in the Vice-Chancellor's court. Wood notes succinctly in his Journal: 'Nov.16, Wednesday, received a citation by the apparator-beadle to appeare in the vice-chancellor's court, Nov.18, Friday' (L & T III, 407).

Wood pleaded not guilty, and over the next months the court met twenty times to hear the pleas and counter pleas. In his defence Wood said that the offending passages had been inserted 'by the printer or printers of the said book without the knowledge and consent of the said Mr Anthony Wood'. When this failed to convince, he offered to print an apology to the effect that 'the author does find that he has been imposed upon by the persons that gave him those accounts. Wherefore he desires the reader to take notice that he does recall those expressions, there being no just grounds for any such insinuations.' Clarendon would have accepted this, if Wood had been prepared to come publicly into the Vice-Chancellor's court to make this submission and had undertaken to pay Clarendon's costs. This Wood refused to do, and so the case dragged on until on 29 July (1693) he was found guilty and was sentenced to pay a fine of forty pounds and to be expelled from the university; and the offending book was to be publicly burnt. 'July 31, about 10 of the clock in the morn, the parator made a fire of two fagots in the Theater [i.e. Sheldonian] yard, and burnt the 2d volume of Ath. Oxon' (L & T III, 429).

This case was to be the ultimate cause of the terrible quarrel between Wood and Aubrey. In November of the previous year, when Clarendon had just initiated his prosecution, Wood had returned to Aubrey Part II of the Lives in a mutilated condition. On the manuscript Aubrey has written:

> Ingratitude! This part the second Mr Wood haz gelded from page 1 to page 44 and pages too are wanting wherein are contained trueths, but such as I entrusted nobody with the sight of but himselfe (whom I thought I might have entrusted with my life). There are severall papers that may cutt my throate. I find too late *Memento diffidere* [remember to distrust] was a saying worthy one of the sages. He hath also embezill'd the index of it – quod N.B. It was stitch't up when I sent it to him. Nov.29. 1692.

The most likely explanation of Wood's extraordinary behaviour is that he panicked when Clarendon brought his action and tore out and destroyed these pages because they included libels on contemporaries which might cause trouble. He was clearly anxious at the reaction to his book and wrote a Preface in which he defended himself against his attackers. Towards the end of November he wrote to Aubrey sending copies of this and asking him to distribute them to his friends in London.

Aubrey's reply begins calmly enough. He has distributed the Prefaces; he gives the reaction of Gadbury to Wood's letter; he reports that Dr Holder is pleased that Wood has 'done him right' against Dr Wallis. Then, almost in passing, he asks him to return the missing pages of his Lives and a scandalous pamphlet satirising the Court, called *Advice to the Painter*. But underlying his apparent insouciance is a note of nervousness; he would have known by now that Clarendon was prosecuting Wood for Scandalum Magnatum and that Wallis was threatening to bring an action; it was imperative that he should have any dangerous material back in his own hands. Before he had despatched the letter he had news from Lord Abingdon which confirmed his worst fears and threw him into despair:

London, Decemb. 3, 1692

Deare Friend,

As soon as I came to Towne, I distributed your Prefaces. But there wanted one: so all but Mr J. Evelyn haz them: and they remember them kindly to you: except Mr Gadbury: I shewed him your letter to me: and he sayes, now you are not able to recall your writing and make him satisfaction. He shewed me his Almanack 1693; where in the 2d page he hath wiped you …

Pray doe me the kindnesse to looke-out my papers (for I find severall missing) and also that piece of a booke (Advice to the Painter) and send them to me. My old Lodgeing is taken-up: and I am not yet settled: so I lye yet at an Inne. Direct your letter to be left with Dr Gale at Paule-schooles. Dr Holder desires to know how Dr J. W(allis) bears it: let me know how your case stands. Pray give Hobbes Leviathan to New-Inne, and my service there.

Decemb. 14

All last weeke I was ill: but on Sunday I went to my Lord Abingdon, who saluted me with a sad aspect. and a sadder Intimation: sc.: That he was exceedingly grieved for the Trouble that was comeing upon me: I was mightily surprized: sayd he, the Earl of Clarendon hath told me, that Mr Wood had confessed to him, that he had the Libell (*Advice to the Painter*) from me: as also the other informations: I doe admire that you should deale so unkindly with me, that have been so faithfull a friend to serve you ever since 1665, as to doe so by me: the Libell was printed, and not uncommon: Could you not have sayd, that you bought it? or had it of George Ent: or somebody that is dead? To be short, my Lord is resolved to ruine me: pray let me know by the next post, what 'tis that you have donne against me, that I may be the better enabled to make my Defence: I must be faine to fly some whither ere long: but nothing grieves me more than that I shall not be able to see my Booke ⌜*Monumenta Britannica*⌝ printed. I much feare I shall never see you, or Oxford again:

so I desire you as a dying person, to looke out my papers for me and send them to Dr Gale, who is my faithfull friend. My heart is ready to breake ... Thus hoping to heare from you presently, I rest

Yours, J. Aubrey.

As to that of Judge Jenkins, I told you, I could attest it from his own mouth. (Tanner 456a, 41)

Abingdon's warning to Aubrey was a cruel joke, as Aubrey later learnt; Wood had not betrayed him to Clarendon. But Aubrey was already afraid that Wood might do so and his fears were not unjustified considering Wood's defence that 'the Author had been imposed upon by the persons who gave him those accounts'; it would have been quite natural for Clarendon to press Wood to give him the source of this material.

Wood replied with an undated letter in which he stoutly denied betraying Aubrey:

Sir,

I have received your letter and thank you for your paines in doing what I desired [i.e. distributing the Preface].

As for the book concerning the *Advice to the Painter*, this is to Assure you in the name of God that I did once see it in the hands of Mr Charles Peroy and if I mistake not in those of George Ent, and am so great a stranger to Henry Earl of Clarendon that I never yet spoke a word to him, nor ever wrote any letter or note to him, nor ever yet saw him except at a distance; of which I am now ready to take my oath in any court of Judicature – therefore I pray rest satisfied as to that matter, and acquaint the noble Earl of Abingdon of it. (F45, 208)

This was all very well, but Wood had still not sent him the missing pages of *Brief Lives* and Aubrey's fears were not entirely allayed.

He next wrote to Wood in April (1693), in ill health and beset by difficulties; the lawsuit between Matthew Kent and his brother William was threatening, he was trying to publish the *Monumenta Britannica* by subscription; he had been attacked and wounded by thieves in March ('March 20, 1693, about 11 at night robbed and 15 wounds in the head' (Auto)); and in April he had a severe attack of gout, which 'nearly carried me away'. The last misfortunes had made him postpone visits to his cousin Elizabeth Freeman and Dr William Holder in Hertfordshire. Considering his situation and Wood's behaviour, Aubrey's letter is extraordinarily restrained and friendly, making only a passing reference to Wood's continued failure to restore the missing pages:

London, April 4, 1693

Mr Wood,

I told you I was invited into Hartfordshire, to Dr Holder (who remembers him kindly to you) and my cousin Freeman, Sir J. Aubrey's sister and his neighbour. I have been here since before March: but never so entangled and ingaged in businesse in my life: and partly in publishing my Booke. I am exceedingly obliged to my old acquaintance Mr J. Dreyden [= Dryden] for his friendly advice and recommendation; he would have his Bookeseller print it, but HE will print only Plays and Romances. So I am advised to do it by Subscriptions, which doe begin pretty luckily. If you can doe me any help in it, it will be kindly donne by you.

I writ to you to send me the papers that you tooke out of my Collection of Lives, and send them to Dr Gale: but he haz heard nothing of them. March 20 I lighted upon Thieves that robbed and wounded me sorely. I kept my Chamber a weeke: and have since then been in a course of Physic, els I had been in Hartfordshire, but intend (God willing) to be there and at Cambridge the later end of next week, where I shall be glad to serve you.

I have been but thrice to the Royal Society since I saw you. People are shy and afrayd to speake freely to me concerning your booke least I should tell you of it. The Peeres (I can tell) are offended at your liberty, be it true or false. Mr Evelyn desired you to send him what you writ of him before you printed it: and takes it unkindly that you did not doe it; but he sayes, you call him a great Virtuoso: and he had rather you had called him Coxcomb ...Your copies are almost all sold, I heare.

I have more to write to you but I am weary with physick: and will let it alone till my next letter, which will be about the end of this month.

Vale, tuissimus, JA (F51, 5)

Chapter XVI

The Quarrel 1693–94

WOOD, TO WHOM AUBREY HAD ENTRUSTED most of his manuscripts, had proved singularly unreliable and in June (1693) Aubrey decided at last to deposit all his writings in the Ashmolean Museum forthwith. He had been planning to do this for five years, but, for fear of offending Wood, he had shilly-shallied. He now acted decisively without informing Wood of his decision and wrote to Tanner telling him to keep it a secret:

1 June 93

Sr,

I have delivered this day at the Saracens head to Mr More the Carrier over against All Soules College a box of manuscripts directed to you, and delivered the key inclosed in a letter to you. I give thankes to God, that have given me such faithful friends as your self and Mr Gibson and Mr Llwyd. You will see by the Lives how much I have obliged my friend Anthony. But I would beseech you to keep it as a Secret that I have sent them: for it would exasperate Mr Wood who may doe me a great mischief, if he should betray me: of which there is suspicion. I would have them deposited (when you have cast your eie on them) in the secret custody of my worthy friend Mr Llwyd, for there are secrets in these Lives which I doe not desire to be exposed to common view until I am dead. When you have donne with my Wiltshire Antiquies, I would have them deposited with Mr Llwyd: and think it fitt that when my brother shall peruse them, that he gives his Bond for the re-delivery of them: for he is almost as tenacious as Anthony ... God blesse you and the rest of my friends of Queens and Jesus College,

Yours, J. Aubrey. (Tanner 25, 49)

Aubrey eventually set out for Hertfordshire on 20 July. He first visited his cousin Elizabeth Freeman and went on to Therfield to stay with Dr William Holder. Aubrey arrived at Therfield at the end of July and from there they proceeded together to Cambridge, where they had a lively stay. By the end of August he knew of the sentence passed on Wood, for back in London he wrote to Tanner: 'At Cambridge I read the fate of our friend Anthony in the Gazette at the Coffee House, and the Heads of Houses are offended with him' (Tanner 25, 82; 30 August 1693). In October Aubrey paid a short visit to Oxford during which he missed Llwyd, who was in Wales, and, significantly, hardly spoke to Wood; from Oxford he went on to Lavington to stay with the Earl of Abingdon. From Lavington he wrote to Wood, bringing him up to date on what had occurred since April, when he last wrote to him, and giving a long and rambling account of the mixed reception Wood's book had received in Cambridge, Hertfordshire and London:

> Lavington Octob.21, 1693
>
> Deare Friend,
>
> I am sorry I was enforced to make so short a stay at Oxford, that I could not have more conversation with you: So I must give you a History of my selfe; viz: after my recovery of my wounds by the thieves I fell most extremely ill of the Goute, for 2 moneths: above halfe the time kept my bed: it almost carried me off: then I tooke the fresh aire, and good entertainment in Hartfordshire at my Cosen Freemans, married to Sr John A[ubrey]'s sister, and Dr Holder, who carried me to Cambridge and brought me acquainted with the Heads of Houses, who kindly entertained me: the news of your Booke I found there in the Gazette: but which I admire at, very few there read your Booke: I told them, 'tis pitty some body does not doe the like for Cambridge: they slighted the proposal, as a useless Learning. They are excellent Philologists etc but, the worst Antiquaries, that I ever conversed with. I had the honour to be acquainted with a matter of 3 Bishops: but both Bishops and Clergie, except the Bishop of London, whom I saw every day (half a mile from Dr Holder) **are spightfull at your great Labours**: I am not acquainted with the London Ministers, but I believe the same humour reignes amongst them all; but on the other side, all the gentry of Hartfordshire (and 'tis very full) **mightily applaud your Book** as most of the Royal Society, except Grandees ... I have here retirement and leisure enough, and have read over Mr Locks book [John Locke, *On Education*, 1693]: but when I come to London I shall be ready to sinke under the trouble I am comeing in, viz. Mr Kent and my brother are up to the eares in Chancery, and I shall be drawn-in: but though my brother hath not been so kind to me as he ought to have been: for he might have had Chalke Farm, now let for £250 per annum, yet when I come upon my oath, I must doe him right though to my owne hiderance ... I forgot to tell you that I just called upon Mr Coley as I was goeing out of Towne; and he is very angry with you, because you terme *Astrologers Conjurers* ... I thinke the time long before I come to Oxon. (F51, 6)

Wood was now a deeply embittered man and his behaviour was

becoming more and more unpredictable; he was filled with pent-up rage against the world, which he was soon to pour out on his most faithful friend and helper. It may have been at this time that he added to his journal the notorious description of his first meeting with Aubrey (see pages 17); in this, he says: '(Aubrey) would stuff his many letters sent to AW with fooleries, and misinformation, which sometimes would guide him into paths of errour.' He may have persuaded himself that Aubrey was responsible for the misfortune he had brought upon himself by libelling Clarendon. He began to abuse Aubrey throughout Oxford, as Aubrey complained to Llwyd the following year: 'He speakes ill of me and bespatters me wherever he goes' (Ashmole 1814, 116).

Aubrey, whose patience and good nature were almost inexhaustible, was getting to the end of his tether, and his next letter to Wood is unusually sharp in tone. The previous year Wood had asked Aubrey to return all his letters, some of which contained material which might be dangerous to him if the publication of his book stirred up trouble; Aubrey had duly returned all but a few which he could not find. Wood had now asked for these missing letters; Aubrey replied asking Wood to return his own letters and to restore the pages he had cut out from his collection of letters (A12, 13); he had sent this collection to Wood in April 1690, and when Wood returned it, ten pages were missing. For a second time Wood had mutilated one of Aubrey's manuscripts; we must suppose that either the letters he had cut out seemed to threaten him in some way, or he kept them as material for his third volume of *Athenae Oxonienses.* In any case Aubrey could scarcely disguise his hurt and anger:

London, St John's Day(= 27 Dec) 1693

Mr Wood,

I returned to London with the Earl of Abingdon 10 dayes since ...

I have not above half a dozen of your letters, which at present I cannot come at. I sent all the [other] letters before. I expect that you should deliver my letters to me. About March I intend to be at Oxford for a month, and desire you to restore the pages you have cutt out of my Collections and then you may peruse the rest: Mr Lloyd [Llwyd] tells me you have not restored them as yet. I wish you a happie New Yeare and am your faithfull friend,

Jo Aubrey. (F39, 442)

Despite the courteous tone of its ending, the letter shows that Aubrey is deeply wounded by Wood's behaviour and that their long friendship is threatening to dissolve.

This is confirmed by a letter he wrote to Llwyd the same day:

London, St Johns Day (= 27 Dec)1693

Mr Llwyd,

I returne my thankes for yours of Dec.4 ...

I am sorry for and admire at Mr Wood's rough dealing with me, who have been and am so kind to him: I have writt to him this day, that if he will returne the Ten sheets which he hath cutt out of my Collection of letters, that he may have the perusall of the rest: otherwise not; and he writes to me to send him all his letters to me (which are not above 6 or 7); I returned to him about a yeare since a matter of 20 yeares letters or more: I must expect the like returne from him of my owne letters. (Ashmole 1814, 114)

Wood meanwhile continued to work on the third volume of *Athenae Oxonienses* and needed Aubrey's manuscripts, especially the *Brief Lives*, all of which Aubrey had placed in the Ashmolean the previous June. In a thoroughly disingenuous letter of 6 February (1694) he demands access to them again, pretending that he needs them to write an account of Aubrey; he represents himself as the injured party and still has a list of queries for Aubrey, as if he had done him no wrong:

I am drudging about the 3d vol. of *Ath. et Fasti Ox.* and think to bring in severall living writers, especially the seniors, among which is yourself, but the title of the booke which you are about to publish I know not – therefore let me have the exact title – you have taken away your other MSS and Collections, and how do you think that I am able to set downe the right titles of these your Collections except you send me them, or else that I may see them? ... I had prepared 20 questions in writing against your sayd comings from Lavington, but you gave me the slip. (A13, 267)

Wood knew very well the title of the book Aubrey was trying to have published (*Monumenta Britannica*); Aubrey had kept him in touch with all developments in this matter. His expostulations are simply a bait to persuade Aubrey to lend him his manuscripts again so that he could use them for his own purposes.

In his next letter to Wood, Aubrey writes as if nothing untoward had happened and says that he intends to visit him in Oxford when he is staying with Sir John Aubrey at Boarstall (F39, 440; 22 April 1694). He was delayed in London and did not get to Boarstall until August. The visit to Wood in Oxford was not a success; Wood was unkind and choleric, and on 2 September Aubrey, still at Boarstall, wrote a letter which precipitated the last and most violent stage of the quarrel. In this he pours out all his unhappiness and hurt at the way Wood has treated him, but even in this letter he invites him to spend a day with him at Boarstall, and ends as warmly as ever:

Borstale. Sept.2d, 1694

Mr Wood!

I thought I would have heard from you ere this time. I have been ill ever since I came from Oxford, till within 5 dayes: of a surfeit of Peaches etc. so that I was fain to send to Kitt White for a good lusty Vomit. I could not eate a bitt of flesh for six dayes, but abstinence hath pretty well settled me again. Your unkindness and choleric humour was a great addition to my ilnes. You know I allwayes loved you and never thought I tooke paines enough to serve you: and I was told by severall at Oxford, and so the last yeare, that you can never afford me a good word. I desired you to give to the Museum my draughtes of Osney, which cost me xxs when I was of Trin. Coll: ... also I desired you to give the Entertainment of the Queen (Elizabeth) at Bushells Rocks (Oxford, 1636): your Nephews and Nieces will not value them. You have cutt out a matter of 40 pages out of one of my volumes, as also the Index (was ever any body so unkind?), and I remember you told me comeing from Hedington, that there were some things in it that **would cutt my throat**. I thought you so deare a friend that I might have entrusted my life in your hands: and now your unkindenes doth almost break my heart. If you will returne those papers to me and the other 3 things to the [Museum], you may then have the Lives.

I should be glad <if you would come to Boarstall>; you shall be heartily welcome and I will <show you> a booke of this house, in parchment, donne in Henry VI and <a lease?> of this Estate granted by Edward Confessor. I would have you come the next weeke, for ... a fortnight hence Sir J. Aubrey goes into Glamorganshire and will have me with him ... You cannot imagine how much your unkindness vext and discomposed me. So God bless you.

Tuissimus, J.A.

...I thinke I told you, that my Lord Abingdon told me, that my Lord Clarendon never sayd any such thing, but he onely spoke it me to banter me and putt me into a fright.

I would have you come as early as you can, because of perusing the MSS and seeing the gardens, for the afternoon will be taken up with good fellowship. (Ballard 14, 155 – MS damaged towards the end)

The same day Aubrey wrote to Llwyd, who by now had replaced Wood as his chief Oxford friend and confidant:

Borestall, Sept 2d, 1694

Mr Llwyd,

I would desire your prudent and friendly advice and Mr Tanners.

Mr Anth Wood is peevish and froward and angry with me, that he hath not my Lives. He is writing of a 3d volume, where he sayes he will make honourable mention of me: but he speakes ill of me and bespatters me wherever he goes: and hath betrayed me to Dr Plott, who is angry with me: but I value not his pride nor his tuft Gowne, nor his Hornes. Mr Wood haz cutt out of one of my volumes ten leaves or more and the Index and keepes it by him: and sayd there are some things that will cutt my throat. I thought I might have trusted my life in his hands; he hath also 3 draughtes of the Ruines of Osney-Abbey which cost me XXs when I was at Trin. Coll: and the Entertainment of the Queen at Bushells Rock … which was given to my Grandfather, which I have ten times over desired of him to putt into the Museum: for when he dies, it will be lost, and torne by his Nieces children.

Now if I could gett out of his handes those papers which he cutt out and the 2 other things, I could be contented he should have perusall of my Ideas: if he have them not, he will abuse me and berate me damnably in his next volume. All that I desire is for good; I grow old, and have to make my owne hands my Executors.

Sir Jo Aubrey and my Lady treat me with all imaginable kindnesse and respect and will have me downe in Wales with him till next summer, and will at his owne cost and charges have my *Templa Druidum* <printed>. The *Templa Druidum* will recommend the rest and pay for the 2d part of the *Monumenta Britannica*, and the 2d for the third. (Ashmole 1814, 116)

The letter shows a turmoil of emotions in Aubrey's mind: anger at Wood's monstrous behaviour, bitter hurt at the betrayal of their friendship, and self-pity ('All that I desire is for good; I grow old …'). But he is as resilient as ever, grateful for the kindness Sir John is showing him in his trouble and optimistic about yet another scheme for the printing of *Monumenta Britannica.*

Aubrey would still have been glad to resolve all differences, if Wood would meet him. The next day he wrote to him again with a more explicit invitation to dine at Boarstall and warning him not to come the day Sir William Glyn was to dine there:

Borstall, Sept. 3, 1694

Mr Wood,

I sent a letter lately to you and desired you to come hither to dinner where you should be very welcome, and see the Antiquities and MSS of this old seate. This is to acquaint you that either next Fryday or Saterday Sir William Glyn and his brother and Mr McKennett dine here who would not looke upon you with a good eie. Any day else Sr John and I shall be glad to see you.

Yours, JA.

Wood did not accept this overture but wrote on 15 September a cold and offensive letter instructing Aubrey to meet him incognito and alone at an ale-house near Boarstall:

Sat. Sept.15

Mr Aubrey,

Next Munday about two in the Afternoon I shall be at Beckley about 2 or 3 miles this side of Boarstall, and therefore this is to desire you that you would take a horse and come by your selfe there to meet me at an Alehouse called the Earle of Abendon's Armes.

I shall bring some queries with me for you to do at London for me when you goe to that place.

I perceive that you will not come to Oxon before you goe to London, or if you doe, you will not call upon me, and therefore I had as good be sure of something.

Last year you slipt from Boarstall to Ricot and I did not see you, and so you may do the same now. If you bring any body with you, let him only be a servant, because I have several things to say to you.

A.W.

If I am not at Beckley before you, make no noise in enquiry after me, nor name my name. (Tanner 456a, 45)

It looks as if Wood intended to administer a browbeating which he did not want others to witness ('I have several things to say to you'), and yet he will come armed with queries, still confident that Aubrey will do more research for him. But before he had despatched this letter, he heard that he was too late; Aubrey would have left Boarstall before Monday. And so he enclosed a new letter in which he wrote what he had intended to say to Aubrey, an outpouring of venom, in which he raked over all his imagined grievances against Aubrey:

Sept.15,1694

Mr Aubrey,

Since my writing the enclosed I received a Letter from you to tell me that you go to Ricot on Sunday: so my journey to Beckley is stopt.

I must tell you that in your letter of 3 Dec.1692 you say thus: – 'All this week I was ill, but on Sunday I went to Lord Abingdon, who saluted me with a sad Aspect and sadder intimation': *scl.* that he was exceedingly grieved for the trouble that was coming upon me – I was mightily surprised – said he, 'the Earl of Clarendon hath told me that Mr Wood had confessed to him that he had the Libell (Advice to the Paynter) from me, as also other informations' – then you go forward thus without examining the matter, whether it be so or no – 'I do admire that you should deale so unkindly with me that have been so faithfull a friend to you ever since 1665 as to do so by me. The Libell was printed and was common: could you not have said that you bought it? or had it of George Ent, or somebody that is dead?' – and so you go forward to plague and disturb my thoughts without examination. At length when you came to towne an yeare after you told me it was a *Banter*. Now I appeale to all the world, whether this was not an unworthy thing in you as to these particulars, first, that which was bad, you let me know it in your letter to disturb my thoughts and rest: but that which proved good (the Banter) you never did let me know it by your letter to comfort my thoughts, only by word of mouth a yeare after, and that by accident.

Another thing since this happens that when I was in your company last at Oxon you told me I had gelt your book, and so in your most wicked and silly letter of 2 of Sept. to tell me so againe, as you did last week in another letter to Mr Llwyd of the Musaeum and perhaps to others.

Now I must let you know that before you disturb my mind by word of mouth and by letters, especially that rascally letter that had been soaked in a bucket of ale, you should have examined the matter and brought the book with you to shew me where the Leaves were cut out, and prove them to be cut out, but this you have not done, but go in with stuff and tattle to abuse without end, before I can know whether the matter be true, or whether such a thing be done.

Another thing is that when a suite was commenced against me by the Earl of Clarendon, your pure spirit was so much affrighted, that after about 20 yeares acquaintance, you took away your books in your Kodpiece (and) left your friend, to seek and shift for your self.

You talk of friendship and acquaintance ever since 1665, and now when a little affliction comes upon our friend, you leave him. – Is this handsome? Suppose your brother or any body else goes to law with you, must I therefore leave you? Must I forsake you? and afterwards terrifie you with unworthy letters relating to the Earl of Abingdon and Cutting out leaves out of my books – Have not my troubles been great enough but you must trouble me with newe? *Apage*! [Away with you!].

Twenty yeares agoe you left in my hands Hobbs Leviathan, which I tooke for a gift: Now at last you take it from me and give it to New inn (Hall) Library; which they will not take. Doe you think that it is a book for young students to study in? No, rather to make them Hobbists, and confound them – you think you have shew'd your selfe very wise in this matter.

There is a little pamphlet of a sheet of paper called Bushells rock, I think, – this with the prospect of Osney which is printed in *Monasticon Anglicanum*, I have had as long, and now they must be given to the Musaeum – this is like a child, *give a thing and take a thing* -

You told me in a former letter that Sr Will. Waller died 9 Sept 1669 and lies buried in the new chappell in Westminster ... – many such things you have deluded me with

> I have several Queries to put in your hands when you come to Oxford, some of which have laid here above twelv month, in expectation of your then coming: but fearing that you will not come, I will send them to you in London at Allhallows tyde, and shall direct them to your lodging in Dirty Lane.
>
> Farewell, and be wise, study not to disturbe people with Letters and reports, before you examine matters – you were found faulty in my Lord of Abendons [= Abingdon's] business and so you may as to gelding and cutting out leaves. (Tanner 456a, 48)

This letter, try as one may to be fair to Wood, is utterly indefensible. The one true grievance he had was that Aubrey had forgotten to tell him sooner that Abingdon's report about Clarendon was banter. He does not deny that he had gelded *Brief Lives* but puts up a smoke-screen of casuistry. It is hardly true that Aubrey deserted Wood when Clarendon brought in his action; there was nothing Aubrey could do to help and he naturally tried to avoid being involved, especially in view of Wood's defence, that he had been 'imposed upon by the persons who gave him this information'. As for the prospects of Osney, Aubrey had asked more than once that Wood should return them when he had finished with them and Wood had assured him that he would do so (e.g. Wood – Aubrey F45, 171, 6 February 1674; Wood acknowledges the receipt of the prospect of Osney Abbey and other papers, 'all of which I shall safely keep and restore at your command'). Finally, Wood accuses Aubrey of deluding him with misinformations; in fact Aubrey went to endless trouble to give accurate answers to Wood's queries and Wood was clearly pushed to find any evidence of inaccuracy, judging from the examples he dredged up. Yet even in this offensive letter Wood still has the effrontery to propose to give Aubrey another list of queries. He could scarcely have written a more malicious and hurtful letter.

Chapter XVII

The Reconciliation 1694–95

Aubrey could not bring himself to reply to Wood's explosion of bile until the following March. But he was incapable of bearing malice and in October he wrote a letter to Llwyd which shows that he would still like to be reconciled with Wood and would continue to answer his queries:

> Lavington, Octob.10,1694
>
> Sir,
>
> I intended to have spent 10 or 14 days at Oxford to enjoy my ingeniose and deare friends. But my Lord Abingdon would have me with him into Wiltshire and carry me hence to London, where I shall be until about the sitting of Parliament ...
>
> Before one of my stitched collections of Lives, I wrote a sheet of paper, A. Wood's ungratefull dealings with me to geld ten sheets (as appeared by the pages) as also the Index. I desire you to lay aside that sheet, which (though true) would make him angry. Remember me kindly to him and tell him shortly after my return to London I will answer his Queries. (Ashmole 1814, 117)

Llwyd did not 'lay aside the sheet'; it still stands before the second part of *Brief Lives* (see page 140).

On 2 March after a long illness Aubrey at last roused himself to write to Wood. He first, as he had promised, answers his queries, but ends with a moving rebuke:

> I have been ill of a great cold ever since St Paule's Day [= 25 January] and have been but a weeke abroad. Your angry letter did very much discompose me and add to my illness ... I have been ever ready to serve you: but have gott neither thankes nor credit by it. I wish you well and rest
>
> Your faithfull friend, JA. (F39, 450; 2 March 1695)

In June Aubrey paid a short visit to Oxford, which he had to cut short owing to business in London; during this visit the seeds of a reconciliation with Wood may have been sown, for he wrote the next month a short letter answering queries and promising to send the rest 'when I write to Mr Llwyd. I cannot now read because of the Mist which comes over my eies ever since I left Oxon' (F39, 452; 18 July 1695). He wrote to Llwyd the same day with a fuller account of the failure of his eyesight.

By August the correspondence between Aubrey and Wood appears to have been resumed almost on its old footing; Aubrey sent a longish letter on 11 August writing 'by guess'; in this, he rambles on in his old way and ends 'Tuissimus' (your dearest friend):

London, Aug.11,1695

My old Acquaintance,

My eies are hardly any thing mending but I can write by guess ... Dr Goodall would have you undertake the Antiquities of Cambridge. He tells me he hath an interest with halfe the Heads of Houses of the University ... Mr President of St John's is now pretty well recovered, and goes to Oxford on Monday next. I told him I would have a Fayre in that lovely pleasant Wood (Bagley Wood) in the Summer-time: for Finery etc. It would certainly concenter all the young people of both sexes 20 miles around.

A letter from Wood survives, which must be dated 15 August, in which he gives some characteristically brusque advice on cures for Aubrey's eye trouble: 'You are to make in one of your shoulders, or between your shoulder and neck-bone on the left side, an issue that in a quarter of an yeares time will cleare your head; or else you must keep your breach open with pills; or els lay playsters of Mastick to your Temples, and leave off sleeping upon a Bed after dinner, or else you'l never be well.' He also gives some information on a 'Chalybiate' spring in Bagley Wood which Aubrey had discovered on his way to Oxford the previous April ('it is disliked because it does not run') (A13, 26). We have Aubrey's reply to this:

London, Sept 2, 1695

Mr Wood,

I received your very kind and obligeing latter of Aug.15. I thank you for your Receipt and Advice; my eies mend but slowly.

There follow answers to Wood's queries and more discussion of medicinal springs, ending 'Tuissimus, J.Aubrey'. In a P.S. he adds: 'On Munday I am for Llanthrithed with Sir J. Aubrey. I hope to see you next May if I live so long.' (F51, 11)

This was the last exchange of letters between Aubrey and Wood, and it is good to find that their long correspondence ends on a friendly note. Wood died on 28 November from a total suppression of the urine, defiant to the last; when he met an acquaintance, Dr Robert South, and told him of his illness, South heartlessly replied that if he could not make water, he must make earth; Wood hurried home and wrote South's life, including the remark: 'It was South's custom to suffer neither sacredness of place nor solemnity of subject to restrain his vein of humour' (L & T iii, 497). He refused until the last to admit that he was in danger and kept his journal until a fortnight before he died. When Dr Charlett heard he was ill and that there was no hope of his recovery, he hastened to see him and persuaded him to prepare for death. He made a will, leaving all his papers to the university and appointed Charlett and Tanner his executors. He took the sacrament and 'died in the communion of the church of England'. 'His behaviour was very well during his illnesse; was very Patient and Quiet, especially towards the latter end; he askt Pardon of all that he had injured; and desired the Prayers of all the Publick Congregations' (Charlett to Archbishop Tenison, 1 December 1695; L & T iii, 497–9).

We have seen that Wood suffered a change of character when he became deaf in 1670 (this disaster 'made him exceedingly melancholy and more retir'd' (L & T ii, 164); and after the troubles occasioned by the publication of his History (1674) and the hostile reception of the work to which he had devoted his life, he became more eccentric and unpredictable. This deterioration accelerated as he was suspected in Oxford of being a papist and he became increasingly isolated and unpopular. By the time of the quarrel, he was embittered and perhaps slightly crazed.

Tanner was Wood's literary executor and in 1713 published a third volume of *Athenae Oxonienses*, about 500 more Lives.

Aubrey survived Wood by only eighteen months. Despite deteriorating health and poor eyesight, he remained active, working now on the *Miscellanies*, a 'Collection of Hermitick Philosophy', i.e. works on the occult. This was the only one of his works to be published in his lifetime (1696) and although it was republished several times and contains some fascinating material, it can hardly have done his reputation as a scholar much good. He continued to write cheerfully to his many friends until the year of his death, e.g. to Llwyd from Llanthrydid where he was staying with his cousin Sir John Aubrey:

Llanthridid Oct.29 1695

Mr Llwyd,

I am extremely caressed here by my Noble Chief Sir J.A. where I am treated with all the varieties the sea and land affords: but I declare I am near so well pleased with a College commons in your good company. In the afternoon we shove the Tankard and the Bottle: one to another in the bond of Peace and frequently drink to your good health ...

And to Hooke:

Llanthridid, Nov.6,1695

Honoured Sir,

I give you my hearty thanks for all your favours and kindness to me. I am, I thanke God, in good health: and want nothing but your good company and our Wednesday meetings at Gresham College.

His last surviving letter is to Llwyd (26 January 1697), whom he asks to give his *Remaines of Gentilisme* to Dr Charleton to revise and tells him to have the manuscript of the *Idea of Education* ready for him when he visits Oxford later, since he intends to transcribe it. He died on 7 June 1697 in Oxford on his way to visit Lady Long and was buried in the church of St Mary Magdalen in Cornmarket.

Aubrey devoted his life to the advancement of learning; his ideas were seminal in several spheres – in the collection and preservation of folklore, in the study of British place names, in work on the chronology of architecture and handwriting, and above all in archaeology. All these apparently disparate efforts formed part of what he considered his mission in life – to preserve the past from 'the teeth of Time'. His endless researches on behalf of Wood may be considered part of the same mission; when he took to biography himself, he considered this 'perhaps one of the usefullest pieces that I have scribbled'; for

> as with the light after sunset – at which time clear; by and by *crepusculum* [twilight]; then total darkness – in like manner is it with matters of antiquitie. Men thinke, because every body remembers a memorable accident shortly after 'tis donne, 'twill never be forgotten, which for want of registring, at last is drowned in oblivion. Which reflection haz been a hint, that by my meanes many antiquities have been reskued and preserved ... or els utterly lost and fogotten. (A9, 29).

He never completed anything he had undertaken and his manuscripts are all chaotic, so filled with additions and corrections that, as Wood warned him, they were virtually unintelligible ('My Minutes were so confused and so interlined (as you say) that had I not donne in my lifetime, they would have signified nothing' (F39, 386; 29 June 1689). This was partly due to external circumstances ('a strange fate that I have laboured under never in my life to enjoy one entire moneth or 6 weekes of otium for contemplation' (Auto), partly from the very copiousness of his ideas, which inspired him to start a new work before he had finished the old, most clearly seen in his embarking on *Brief Lives* before he had finished the Life of Hobbes.

There may be a third and more profound reason, rooted in his psyche.

He suffered from frequent mood swings, alternations between periods of 'lethargy', occasioned, as he thought, by the malign influence of the planets, and periods of irrational high spirits. Thus in April 1673 he was in a deep depression during which he repeatedly postponed his departure for Surrey; this lasted at least until 17 June when he wrote to Wood: 'I am not yet free from the malicious aspects of Saturn: the delicate aire and diversion of Surrey will cure my lassitude of spirit (I hope).' But by 10 August, writing from Sussex, he was in a state of euphoria, delighted by his pilgrimage through Surrey and making highly unrealistic plans for the future.

Similarly, in the summer of 1687 he was in a deep depression brought on by the death of his mother and his quarrel with William over the disposal of Chalke. But on 4 August he set out on an excursion to Yorkshire from which he returned in a state of high excitement, writing a lively and cheerful letter to Wood in which he says he has embarked on a new work (*Villare Anglicanum*) and plans to write Natural Histories of Gloucestershire, Monmouthshire, Flyntshire and Surrey.

External factors may account for his depressions but the following 'highs' seem irrational and unrelated to circumstances. When he was forced to 'abscond as a banish'd man' and took refuge in his 'mew' at Broad Chalke, he wrote to Wood, 'I have now these three weekes more enjoyed my selfe than I have in the 19 yeares since my father dyed.'

And again the following year, when everything seemed against him, he wrote from Hethfield, 'I have not enjoyed myselfe so much for 20 yeares.' Such mood swings, in which lethargy alternates with bouts of intense creative energy when anything seems possible, might be taken as evidence of manic depression. This diagnosis is supported by his behaviour towards his brother William between 1686 and 1691. He had never got on well with him, but suddenly William became 'my Tygre brother', threatening to devour him. Aubrey's account of subsequent events in his letters to Wood is completely at variance with the picture which emerges from William's letters; while Aubrey portrays himself as the victim of William's fury and unkindness, William's letters show himself as courteous, affectionate, and grateful despite Aubrey's monstrous behaviour towards him. Either Aubrey is lying to Wood or he was living in a world of illusion. All that we know of Aubrey shows that he was not a liar and we can only conclude that he was suffering from paranoia, which lasted from the summer of 1688 until the autumn of 1691, when he wrote a letter to Wood in which he showed a more realistic view of events and even a touch of remorse: 'My brother has been unkind to me and (God forgive me) I have undonne him and my selfe' (F39, 435; 27 October 1691). Later he seems to have effected a reconciliation with his brother; we may surmise that he came to himself and throwing off this fit of madness saw events as they really were.

It is well known that many manic-depressives are creative people with attractive personalities. Aubrey was well loved by nearly all who knew him, not only by contemporaries such as John Hoskyns and William Petty, who longed for 'Terme because you promise to be here then' (A13, 10: 22 August 1685), but by men of all generations – by Thomas Hobbes, to whom he was related rather as Boswell was to Johnson, or by the young Thomas Pigot, who wrote on one occasion: 'Never was anything so tedious to me as the time which has passed of late; for not having enjoyed your conversation for so long a time, my soul seem'd, as it were imprisoned and grown heavy for want of action' (A13, 127; 25 October 1680).

It is clear that even Wood, a notoriously difficult man, fell under the spell of his personality and the deterioration in their relationship which led to the great quarrel was not occasioned by any failing on Aubrey's part; Aubrey, though deeply hurt, was consistently loyal and ever ready to make things up. Despite the vicissitudes of the last two years, Wood remained 'my deare Friende and old correspondent'; he wrote to Tanner from Llanthridyd:

> I am extremely sorrowful for the death of my deare Friende and old correspondent Mr Anthony Wood: who (though his spleen used to make him chagrin and to chide me), yet we could not be asunder, and he would always see me at my Lodgeing, with his darke Lanthorne, which should be a Relick ... I am glad that you have all his papers and will be faithfull to him and finish what he left undon. (Tanner 24, 108; 19 March 1696)

Appendix I

The Works of Aubrey and Wood

Aubrey's Works

Aubrey made a catalogue of his works for Edward Llwyd, Keeper of the Ashmolean Museum, in 1692; this lists twenty-two works, of which all but six survive; they are now in the Bodleian Library, except for *The Remaines of Gentilisme*, which is in the British Library. None was published in his lifetime except for *The Miscellanies* (1696). In the following list they are arranged in the order of the Bodleian manuscripts and I have added in brackets reference to editions of these works published after his death.

A1 The Natural History of Wiltshire, Part 1
A2 The Natural History of Wiltshire, Part 2

There is a fuller manuscript version in the Royal Society Library (MS92)

(Both Parts published in an abbreviated form by John Britton (1847) and republished by Newton Abbot Press in 1969)

A3 The Wiltshire Antiquities

(= An Essay towards the Description of the North Division of Wiltshire)

This was in two volumes, Liber A and Liber B, but the second was borrowed from the Ashmolean Library by William Aubrey in 1703 and never returned.

(J.E. Jackson, *Aubrey's Wiltshire Collections*, London, 1862)

A4 Perambulation of the County of Surrey

This was published in a revised and augmented form by Rawlinson and Curll in 1718.

(A facsimile edition of this was published by the Dorking Press in 1975 in five volumes)

A5 An Interpretation of Villare Anglicanum

A6 Brief Lives Part 1
A7 Brief Lives Part 2
A8 Brief Lives Part 3
A9 The Life of Hobbes

(Andrew Clark, *Aubrey's Brief Lives*, two volumes, Oxford, 1898. Oliver Lawson Dick, *Aubrey's Brief Lives*, Secker & Warburg, 1949)

A10 An Idea of Education of Young Gentlemen

(J.E. Stephens, *Aubrey on Education*, Routledge, 1972)

A12–13 Letters to Aubrey
A17 Designatio de Easton-Piers
A21 Miscellaneous papers (including *The Country Revell*)
A23 Collectio Geniturarum
A26 Faber Fortunae
T.G.c24 Monumenta Britannica vol. I (formerly A14)
T.G.c25 Monumenta Britannica vol. II (formerly A15)

(A facsimile edition (incomplete) of *Monumenta Britannica* in two volumes was published in 1980/81, editors J. Fowle and R. Legg)

WORKS NOT IN THE BODLEIAN:

The Miscellanies, published 1696; reprinted 1721, 1784, 1857, 1890

(J.Buchanan-Brown, *Three Prose Works*, Fontwell Press, 1972)

The Remaines of Gentilisme and Judaisme: in the British Museum, Lansdowne MS 231. (J. Buchanan-Brown, ibid)

LOST WORKS

A Collection of Divine Dreams
Hypothesis Ethica and Scala Religionis
Villa, or A Description of the Prospects from Easton Piers
A Collection of approved Receipts
Adversaria Physica
An Introduction to Architecture

Wood's Works

Historia et Antiquitates Univ. Oxon 1674

Athenae Oxonienses 1691–2

Wood left all his vast collection of papers to the Ashmolean from where they were transferred to the Bodleian in 1860. These include:

1. His Autobiography from 1632 to 1672 (Rawlinson D 97)
2. Journal Notes from 1657 to 1695 (Rawlinson D 26)
3. Wood F39–45. Seven volumes of letters to and from Wood

1 and 2 are published in A. Clark, *Wood's Life and Times* (Oxford Historical Society, four volumes, 1891–1895)

Appendix II

The Amici

Aubrey made a list of his fourteen closest friends which he added to his autobiographical notes:

Anthony Ettrick (c.1622–1703); a contemporary of Aubrey at Trinity and at the Middle Temple, he was a lifelong friend. He shared Aubrey's interest in antiquities and the occult (see page ?)

John Lydall (see page 9)

Francis Potter (see page 9)

Sir John Hoskyns (see page 7)

Edmund Wyld (see page 27)

Robert Hooke (see pages 10–11)

Thomas Hobbes (1588–1679); philosopher; Leviathan (1651)

Anthony Wood (1632–1695)

Sir William Petty (1623–1687): son of a poor clothier in Hampshire, he went to sea when he was fifteen and then studied in the Jesuit college in Caen. Became a friend of Hobbes in Paris; returned to England and became a Fellow of Brasenose and then Professor of Anatomy. He went to Ireland as physician to General Fleetwood and carried out a survey of all Ireland, for which he was rewarded with vast estates. Back in England he was knighted and was an original Fellow of the Royal Society. He was the founder of the science of statistics and the author of innumerable inventions. He became a close friend of Aubrey, who says of him; 'To be short, he is a person of so great worth and learning, and haz such a prodigious working witt, that he is both fit for, and an honour to, the highest preferment.'

Sir James Long (1617–1692) FRS (see page 70)

Mr Charles Seymour (1621–1665); he was the friend with whom Aubrey was hunting when he discovered Avebury (see page?). He died young and no letters from him survive.

Sir John Stawell (1625–1669): he was at the Middle Temple with Aubrey. One letter from him survives, in which he asks Aubrey to join him on the Salisbury coach: 'I will not permit deniall, let no slovenly, paultry, pitiful excuse be invented.'

Seth Ward (1617–1689); mathematician; Savilian Professor of Geometry at Oxford; elected FRS with Aubrey 1663. Bishop of Salisbury 1667.

Dr William Holder (1616–98); elected FRS in 1663 with Aubrey; rector of Therfield in Hertforshire. Wrote *Elements of Speech* and works on music. Taught a deaf mute to speak, which involved him in controversy with Wallis, who claimed credit for it.

Appendix III

The Preface to Templa Druidum *(Part 1 of* Monumenta Britannica*)*

Part of the beginning of this Preface, on the discovery of Avebury, is quoted on pages 8, 9, 11. We give below its ending, in which Aubrey states his most important conclusion, that the megalithic monuments date from long before the Roman period, and explains his method, based on precise surveys of the monuments themselves and comparison of one with another. This was entirely novel. His comparative method enabled him to show that they dated to before the Danish or Roman invasions; of this he had clear evidence. His theory that they were temples of the Druids, he offers only as a probability. Of recent books on Stonehenge, Inigo Jones (*StoneHeng Restored*, 1655) had argued that it was built by the Romans, and Walter Charleton (*Chorea Gigantum*, 1663) that it was the work of the Danes. Before Aubrey writers had relied mainly on the testimony of such records as there were; but these gave little or no information on the megalithic monuments, so old that 'no Bookes doe reach them'. Aubrey relied on careful inspection and recording of sites (with detailed plans) made on the spot.

> There have been several Bookes writt by learned men concerning Stoneheng, much differing from one another, some affirming one thing, some another. Now I come in the rear of all by comparative Arguments to give clear evidence that those Monuments were Pagan Temples: which was not made-out before, and here also (with humble submission to better judgement) offer a probability that they were Temples of the Druids.
>
> When a Traveller rides along by the Ruines of a Monastery, he knows, by the manner of the building, sc. Chapell, Cloysters etc: that it was a Convent, but of what order (sc. Benedictine, Dominican etc.) it was, he cannot tell from the bare View. So it is cleer that all the Monuments, which I have here recounted, were Temples. Now my Presumption is, that the Druids being the most eminent Priests (or Order of Priests) among the Britaines, 'tis odds, but that these Monuments (sc. Aubury, Stoneheng, Keerig y Druidd etc.) were Temples of the Priests of the most eminent Order, viz. Druids, and it is strongly to be presumed, that Aubury, Stoneheng etc. are as ancient as those times. This Inquiry I must confess is a gropeing in the Dark: but although I have not brought it into a cleer light, yet I can affirm, that I have brought it from utter darkness to a

thin mist: and have gone farther in this Essay than any one before me. These Antiquities are so exceeding old, that no Bookes doe reach them. So that there is no way to retrieve them but by comparative antiquities, which I have writt upon the *Spott*, from the Monuments themselves. *Historia quoquo modo facta bona est* (History is good, however made): and though this be writt, as I rode, at a-gallop; yet the novelty of it, and the faithfulness of the Delivery, may make some emends for the uncorrectness of the stile. The first draft was worn-out with time and handling: and now, me thinkes, after many years lying dormant, I come abroad like the Ghost of one of those Druids.

Index Nominum